DOUBT

THE MADELEINE MCCANN MYSTERY

By Nick van der Leek

Editing and research by Lisa Wilson

Cover design: Nick van der Leek

"They've taken her! They've taken her!"
— <u>Kate McCann shouted these words</u> from the balcony of the apartment[1] of the Ocean Club resort in the Portuguese town of <u>Praia da Luz</u>, May 3rd 2007 at around 22:00

"Had Madeleine been given some kind of sedative to keep her quiet? Had the twins, too?"
— <u>Kate McCann</u>

"From the start a terrible doubt has never left me."
— David Jones, Daily Mail

---

1 According to Kate McCann she ran to the Tapas bar and screamed as soon as her table was in sight. McCann also stresses that what she shouted was: "Madeleine's gone! Someone's taken her!"

Important Note to the Reader:

The Rocket Science books are unique. Throughout this book, the author has provided hyperlinks to relevant resources including documents, photographs and videos to enhance your interactivity with the story.

TABLE OF CONTENTS

~

Introduction

Three-year-old Madeleine McCann, the daughter of two British doctors, disappeared [it was said] from apartment 5A at approximately 21:15 – 22:00 [it was claimed] in the Ocean Club resort in the Algarve region of Southern Portugal, on May 3rd 2007.

British celebrities, millionaires, billionaires, bands, bestselling authors and the world's favourite football stars immediately rallied to the McCann's cause. The Pope and Britain's prime minister offered their support. Films appealing for help in the search for Madeleine were broadcast during the EUFA Cup Final on May 16th, and on the big screen at half time during the FA Cup final three days later.

By June, at a meeting of the G8, the German Justice Minister weighed in. British journalists gave themselves over to tell the McCann's story using the McCann's words and adopting the McCann's tone in their coverage.

Every day for six months straight, British tabloids unvaryingly ran a story about the search for "Maddie" on their front page. Each time they did, circulations increased anywhere between 30 000 and 80 000 copies.

The McCanns, especially between early May 2007 [when Madeleine vanished] and until mid-September [when the Polícia Judiciária named them "arguidos"[2]] actively fed and participated in the feeding frenzy of a ravenous media machine.

---

2 Arguido is the Portuguese term for official suspect.

In one sense a media war erupted with the British tabloids on one side and the Portuguese tabloids on the other. Soon bickering matches erupted between British investigators and their Portuguese counterparts. When Goncalo Amaral, the plucky investigator and former police chief in charge of the investigation criticised British detectives[3] he was promptly fired.

With the Lisbon Summit scheduled for later that same year, the highly- charged highly-politicised case bounced hither and thither, a legal football on a political football field.

The standoff between accused and their accusers devolved as it invariably does in true crime: book wars erupted between the fired lead detective and the prime suspects.

In 2008 Goncalo Amaral published *The Truth of the Lie*. Three years later Kate McCann published her own counter-narrative amid rumours Harry Potter creator J.K. Rowling had helped her write it. It soon had to be clarified that Rowling had no involvement in Kate McCann's book besides sharing the same literary agent.

Libel wars flared up, soon engulfing the tabloids, the McCanns, the Tapas Seven, and in March 2017, twitter users who dared criticise the McCanns.

During the ten years since Madeleine McCann's disappearance, her parents spent eight of them waging a book war against Amaral, attempting at turns to sue and silence Amaral himself, and otherwise to ban his book.

---

3 Goncalo Amaral was fired as lead investigator on October 3rd, 2007 for making the following statement to the media: *"[The British police] have only investigated tips and information developed and worked on for the McCanns, forgetting that the couple are suspects in the death of their daughter Madeleine."*

But if Amaral had lost political support and the backing of his superiors, that didn't mean he didn't have a legal basis or popular support [even in Britain] for his claims.

In May 2016, Britain's <u>internet "trolls" raised over £50,000</u>[4] to pay for an appeal for the retired police officer. Some of the donors to this fund were members of Britain's Metropolitan police 'outraged' by what had happened to the former investigator. <u>The McCanns finally lost their campaign against Amaral on March 23rd, 2017.</u>

Now that <u>the chips have been played to completion</u> by both sides, what do we know for certain? For one thing, we know Madeleine is still missing. What we still don't know is precisely how or why or even whether she disappeared.

So, has nothing changed since May 3rd, 2007? Have we learnt nothing in ten years? <u>Far from it.</u> Despite the absence of a trial, what we have now is a fairly precise version of events from the McCanns themselves [a by-product of their relentless PR] and we know Amaral's counter-narrative [now a legally defensible matter of public record]. The questions that arise from these opposing narratives are dead simple:

Which narrative is more credible?

Which narrator is more credible?

There are also other questions to ask which are perhaps even more troubling, and yet in another sense easier to plumb and probe:

Who actually benefitted from the immense blanket coverage surrounding this case?

---

4 The GoFundMe campaign supporting Amaral was started in Britain by a student and single mother, <u>Leanne Baulch</u> based in Birmingham.

Did Madeleine benefit?

Arguments were fielded at the time that if Madeleine had been abducted, and it was far from certain that she was, that the risk of being associated with *the highest profile missing person in history* would simply not have been worth it. So why did the Madeleine McCann case become the most heavily reported missing-person case in modern history?

What was the motive behind the frenetic publicity?

If money was the motive, if Madeleine had been snatched as part of a botched burglary [the latest theory from British investigators] then why did the burglars make no attempt to claim the £2.5million reward posted nine days after her disappearance?

On the other hand, if neither Madeleine nor her abductor had benefitted from the ongoing media barrage, *then who had*?

Key Individuals

*"It is unbelievable they have been named as suspects
– no-one believes the Portuguese police."*
— Philomena McCann

The ages cited below refer to age on the date of Madeleine's death/ disappearance.

McCann Clan

1. Dr. Gerry McCann. Consultant cardiologist [39], from Rothley, Leicestershire. Father of Madeleine, husband of Kate.

2. Dr. Kate McCann. Part-time GP, former anaesthetist [39], from Rothley, Leicestershire. Mother of Madeleine, wife of Gerry.

3. Madeleine McCann. [3 and eleven months] – victim, missing since May 3rd, 2007, officially presumed dead.[5]

4. Sean McCann. [2 and three months]. Gerry and Kate's son, Madeleine's brother, and Amelie's twin.

5. Amelie McCann. [2 and three months]. Gerry and Kate's daughter, Madeleine's sister, and Sean's twin.

---

5 The McCanns have – to the present day – refused to apply for a death certificate for their daughter.

Extended McCann Family and Support

6. <u>Sandy and Patricia [Trish] Cameron</u>. Trish is Gerry McCann's sister. The Cameron's arrived in Algarve on May 4th, 2007 and left almost two months later in late June. Sandy's name appeared on the Renault Scenic car hire permit. Trish testified for the McCanns in Lisbon. The Camerons have since divorced.

7. <u>John McCann</u> [48], Gerry McCann's brother. Medical representative for AstraZeneca, an International Anglo-Swedish pharmaceutical company headquartered in London. Sales in 2003 totalled $18.8 billion, with a profit before tax of $4.2 billion. AstraZeneca's licensed products have special relevance to Gerry McCann's field: Cardiology. John McCann in 2007 was a co-director of the Find Madeleine Fund.

8. <u>Diane McCann</u>. John McCann's wife, and Gerry McCann's sister in law. She is a school teacher and actively participates in fund-raising. She and John, and their two children, live in Glasgow.

9. <u>Fiona [10] and Gregor</u> [7]. John and Diane McCann's children, niece and nephew to Gerry and Kate, cousins to Madeleine, Sean and Amelie.

10. <u>Philomena McCann</u>. Gerry McCann's sister, high school teacher from Scotland. Often acts as family spokesperson.

11. <u>Anne-Marie Wright</u>. [43] Cousin of Kate McCann and wife of Michael Wright. Lives in Skipton, Yorkshire. The Wrights helped with the search for Madeleine in Algarve, as well as babysat Sean and Amelie when needed.

12. <u>Michael Wright</u>, husband of Anne-Marie Wright. Michael testified for the McCanns in Lisbon. Michael was the co-signatory on the hire car.

13. Katie and Peter Wright. Children of Anne-Marie and Michael. Kate and Gerry McCann are their godparents.

14. <u>Susan and Brian Healy</u>. Mother and father of Kate McCann; grandparents to Madeleine. They live in Liverpool.

15. <u>Nora Paul</u>. Brian Healy's sister, and Kate McCann's aunt. Also, Madeleine's godmother. Lives in Vancouver, Canada.

16. <u>Eileen McCann</u>. Mother of Gerry McCann, was married to [deceased] John McCann. They originally lived in Donegal then moved to Glasgow in 1967.

17. <u>Brian Kennedy</u>. Madeleine's Great Uncle, brother of Kate's mother, Susan. Retired head teacher and resident of Rothley. Appointed co-director to Find Madeleine Fund on May 16th, 2007.

18. <u>Janet Kennedy</u>. Brian's wife and Madeleine's Great Aunt. They went twice a day to the central square of Rothley, the village near Leicestershire, to speak with journalists.

19. Simon and Miriam Cowell. [37] and [29], Simon is the cousin of Kate, and brother of Anne-Marie Wright. They live on the Isle of Man.

20. Lily and Thomas Cowell. [15-months-old] and [6], they are the children of Simon and Miriam Cowell.

21. <u>Sheila Cowell</u>. Kate McCann's aunt and the mother of Simon and Anne-Marie Cowell.

22. <u>Dr. Doug Skehan</u>. Gerry McCann's boss. Cardiologist, Clinical Director and LNR Cardiac Network Clinical Lead at Glenfield Hospital. Marathon runner and charity fundraiser. Skehan's wife, Marcelle [sometimes referred to as Dr. Morris], is a general practitioner. Appointed co-director of Find Madeleine Fund on 16 May 2007. Resigned August 24th, 2010.

23. Peter Hubner. Former hospital consultant in Cardiology and Anaesthetics. Honorary Secretary of the British Cardiovascular

Prevention Society (1988-1992). Appointed co-director of Find Madeleine Fund on May 21st, 2007. He has since resigned.

24. Philip Tomlinson. Lawyer, former HM Coroner for Leicester North. Family links to Leicester County Council. Likely connections within Leicester Police Authority. Appointed co-director of Find Madeleine Fund on 20 June 2007. Resigned and replaced by Jon Corner on January 9, 2008.

25. Michael Linnett. Retired accountant. Appointed co-director of Find Madeleine Fund on August 15, 2007.

26. Esther McVey. Former GMTV presenter [and school friend of Kate McCann]. Trustee and spokeswoman for McCann's Find Madeleine Fund. In 2005, McVey unsuccessfully stood as a Conservative Party candidate for Wirral West in the UK General Election.[6] Law graduate and founder of PR Company 'Making It Ltd' [brand and image management specialists, media strategists, and crisis management specialists. Clients include HSBC. Appointed co-director of Find Madeleine Fund on 20 June 2007. Resigned on 9th January 2008. Replaced by Edward Smethurst.

27. Father Haynes Hubbard and Susan Hubbard. Anglican priest and his wife at the church of Nossa Senhore da Luz, in Praia da Luz.

28. Calum MacRae. [18] started the Find Madeleine website. A policeman's son, MacRae had a team of six people helping with the site, and was paid by donations to the Madeleine Fund.

29. Karen McCalman. Kate's friend from a local mom's group. Lives in East Gascote, Leicestershire. Occasionally babysat Madeleine.

30. Stewart Hillis. Professor of cardiovascular and exercise testing in Department of Medicine and Therapeutics, University of

---

6 McVey succeeded in becoming a Member of Parliament in 2010.

Glasgow. He and Gerry McCann are joint-authors of several medical papers. Hillis also worked with Scotland's football team, providing a link between the team and the Madeleine campaign.

31. Alistair Douglas. Gerry's friend since they were students at Glasgow University.

32. Paul and Kate McIntyre. Friends of Gerry. Paul has known Gerry since they were teenagers. They met through a running club and both attended Glasgow University. Gerry took over Paul's teaching post at Glasgow University after he and Kate returned from New Zealand.

33. Michelle Corner. Wife of Jon Corner, friend to Gerry and Kate.

34. Linda and Mark McQueen. Close friends to Kate and Gerry. Linda and Kate have been friends since childhood. They spoke at 2:00am on the night Madeleine vanished and Linda later went to Portugal to visit Kate. Mark is a teacher and is godfather to Madeleine's brother, Sean. Kate is godmother to the McQueen's daughter, Ellie.

35. Nichola (Nicky) Gill. [39] childhood friend of Kate's. They've known each other since they were six. Nicky is a runner and personal trainer and has helped raised funds for Madeleine's Fund through various races.

36. Jill and Andrew Renwick. Jill and Kate are best friends and the Renwicks acted as media liaisons. Jill spoke to Kate on May 4th at 7am. According to Jill, Kate told her "Help me, please help me. We've been searching all night until 4:30am, and then everybody left us." Jill says the McCanns didn't know what to do, there was only one police officer at the door, so they phoned GMTV.

Suspects

37. <u>Robert Murat</u>. The first official arguido in the case, he lived about 150 yards away from apartment 5A. "Basically, I'm just an ordinary, straightforward guy who's the victim of the biggest f***-up on this planet – if you'll excuse the language." – Daily Mail, June 2, 2007.

38. "<u>Mr. Khaki</u>." At approximately 9:15 PM, on the night of Madeleine's disappearance, Jane Tanner reportedly saw a man in khaki pants carrying a child in his outstretched arms as he hurried down <u>Dr Augusthino da Silva</u>.

39. "<u>Creepy Man</u>." Reportedly seen by Paul Gordon and Gail Cooper the week before the McCanns arrived in Algarve, and reported in News of the World, January 2008.

40. <u>Raymond Hewlitt</u>. Convicted paedophile. After his presence in the Algarve was revealed by Alan and Cindy Thompson, Hewlitt became the lightning rod for speculation in the media

Investigators [Portugal]

41. <u>Goncalo Amaral</u>. Former lead investigator. Removed from investigation on October 2nd, 2007 for criticising the British police. Subsequently wrote a book which was published on July 24th, three days after <u>the case was officially closed</u>.

42. <u>Paulo Rebelo</u>. Amaral's replacement until case was shelved on July 21st, 2008. From that date, Portugal's secrecy laws surrounding the case also lifted and the files were released.

Investigators [Britain]

43. <u>Chief Constable Matt Baggott</u>. Coordinator of British response.

44. <u>Jim Gamble</u>, head of Child Exploitation and Online Protection Centre [CEOP]. Gamble understood that Portuguese police felt

at the time of the investigation they were being condescended to; they felt the British were acting as a "colonial power".

45. Mark Harrison. <u>National search advisor of the NPIA</u>. Harrison organised the search by the world-renowned sniffer dogs on approximately 20 July 2007.

Criminal Profilers

46. <u>Pat Brown</u> [USA]. <u>Brown</u> has appeared on many high-profile programs to provide commentary, profiling and forensic analysis on various cases. She's also written several books including *Killing for Sport: Inside the Minds of Serial Killers* and *The Profiler: My Life Hunting Serial Killers and Psychopaths* along with Bob Andelman. Brown, who has analyzed the McCann case, <u>believes Madeleine is dead</u>.

Tapas Seven and Family

47. <u>Dr. David Payne</u>. [41] Stayed in <u>Apartment 5H</u> on the first floor. <u>Consultant Surgeon Urologist</u> specialising in urological cancers. He was a surgeon at Leicester Royal Infirmary. Last non-family member to positively see Madeleine alive in apartment 5A at 18:30 on May 3rd, 2007.

48. <u>Dr. Fiona Payne</u>. [35] Stayed in <u>Apartment 5H</u> on the first floor. Wife of David Payne. The only couple to have a baby monitor at the Tapas bar that night. She and David stayed at the Algarve for several weeks after Madeleine's disappearance to support Kate and Gerry.

49. Lilly Payne. [2] Daughter of David and Fiona Payne.

50. Scarlett Payne. [11 months] Daughter of David and Fiona Payne.

51. Dianne Webster. [63] Stayed in Apartment 5H on the first floor. Mother to Fiona Payne. Lives in Bedford and worked as a credit manager.

52. Dr. Matthew Oldfield. [37] Stayed in Apartment 5B on the ground floor. He worked with Gerry McCann in Leicester before moving to London. Matthew was last to check on the children, 30 minutes prior to Madeleine being discovered missing, but never looked at Madeleine's bed.

53. Rachael [Mampilly] Oldfield. [36] Stayed in Apartment 5B on the ground floor. Human resources manager living in London.

54. Grace Oldfield. [19 months] Daughter of Matthew and Rachael Oldfield

55. Dr. Russell O'Brien. [37] Stayed in Apartment 5D on the ground floor. Previously lived near the McCanns in Leicester, moved to Devon. Works at the University of Plymouth's Exeter Campus. Friend of David Payne's from school.

56. Jane Tanner. [7] [36] Stayed in Apartment 5D on the ground floor. Marketing Manager at the Exeter Campus. Claims she witnessed abduction by reporting a man in khaki pants carrying a child.

57. Ella O'Brien. [3] Daughter of Jane Tanner and Dr. Russell O'Brien.

58. Evie O'Brien. [1] Daughter of Jane Tanner and Dr. Russell O'Brien.

Media [Britain]

59. David Mills, TV journalist. Original producer of November 2007 Panorama film

---

7 Following Madeleine's "abduction" Russell O'Brien and Jane Tanner, who had lived together but were not married, separated.

60. <u>Jon Corner</u>. Creative director and media production expert for an advertising agency based in Liverpool. Corner recorded one of <u>the first television interviews in August 2007.</u>

61. <u>Clarence Mitchell</u>. McCann family spokesman [Former BBC journalist].

62. <u>Alex Woolfall</u>. Bell Pottinger[8] [a British PR firm] represented the hotel group Mark Warner Ltd. Woolfall dealt with the media for the first ten days. Subsequently, in an "unprecedented" move, the British government sent in press officers, including Clarence Mitchell [then a government employee].

63. <u>Martin Brunt</u>. Sky News. Confronted Brenda Leyland of "trolling" the McCanns shortly before her sudden death.

64. <u>Tracey Kandohla</u>. <u>Freelance writer</u> covering the Midlands for Britain's national newspapers and magazines.

---

8 The capacity for public relations to shape perceptions on a national or international scale should not be underestimated. Bell Pottinger, the same firm hired by Mark Warner Ltd to deal with PR fallout surrounding the incident at Ocean Club has been implicated in shaping the narrative of a corrupt cabal of Indian businessmen, with links to government and the South African president. Bell Pottinger was hired amidst allegations of state capture to "control the narrative" in South Africa. Bell Pottinger was accused of creating a false narrative to distract from the allegations against their clients. Their "deflection campaign" using fake twitter accounts, fake bloggers, bots and commentators was conducted via social media. <u>The public were so incensed by the fake publicity surrounding Oakbay, South Africans eventually marched on the Bell Pottinger offices in London</u>, waving placards of Bell Pottinger's partner with Oakbay, Victoria Geoghegan. This negative backlash <u>prompted the company to break ties with the Guptas and Oakbay</u>. One <u>reputable businessman has described the company</u> as "experts at disinformation."

Media [Portugal and Europe]

65. <u>Nacho Abad.</u> Spanish journalist. On the day that the McCanns gave a press conference at the European Parliament in Brussels, Abad revealed via an anonymous Polícia Judiciária source that Madeleine had asked her mother why she and her brother had been left to cry for so long on the night of May 2nd [the night before she disappeared].

66. <u>Felicia Cabrita</u>. Portuguese investigative journalist, <u>Sol</u>.

67. <u>Margarida Davim</u>. Portugese investigative journalist, Sol.

68. <u>Hernâni Carvalho</u>. Carvalho authored a book on the case, *Maddie 129* with 129 questions.

69. <u>Sandra Felgueiras</u>. Journalist at RTP.

70. <u>Len Port</u>. Algarve author and journalist.

71. <u>Natasha Donn</u>. Journalist for the Algarve Resident.

McCann Legal Representation and Private Investigators

72. <u>Michael Caplan QC</u>. One of the first solicitor advocates in the UK, and the first solicitor from a criminal law background to be made QC. Caplan was an advisor to the McCanns.

73. <u>Edward Smethurst</u>, [38] acted as the McCann's legal coordinator. He's Head of Legal Services for the Latium Group and its related companies owned by Brian Kennedy. He's also a co-director in the Madeleine Fund.

74. <u>Angus McBride</u>. Leading solicitor for the McCanns. Partner at <u>Kingley Napley</u> since 2002.

75. <u>Carlos Pinto de Abreu</u>. The first lawyer to represent the McCanns.

76. Kevin Halligen. Reportedly fleeced the Find Madeleine Fund to the tune of £300,000.

77. Dave Edgar. Head of Alpha Investigation Group (Alphaig Limited). Private detective agency hired by the McCanns.

Sniffer Dogs and Trainer

78. Keela. [7] McCann crime-scene-investigation (CSI) springer spaniel based at South Yorkshire police. Helped police put Trevor Hamilton behind bars in 2006.

79. Eddie. Enhanced-victim-recovery dog (EVRD). Springer spaniel based at South Yorkshire police.

80. Martin Grime. Keela and Eddie's handler.

Ocean Club Staff and Guests

81. John Hill. Director of Mark Warner Ltd.[9] Hill was seconded at midday on May 4th to assist in printing of missing person's leaflets using the Ocean Club's printer and colour copier [a Toshiba].

82. Catriona Treasa Sisile Baker. Childcare worker, Ocean Club, Madeleine's babysitter.

83. Silvia Baptista. Maintenance and Service Manager.

84. Emma Louise Knight. Hotel manager.

85. Helder Jorge Samaio Luis. Receptionist on duty on the night of 3rd May, 2007.

86. Lindsay Johnson. Crèche manager.

---

9 Mark Warner Ltd was the tour operator used by the Tapas Nine to book their holiday to the Algarve.

87. Georgina Jackson. <u>Tennis coach</u>.

88. Dan Stuk. Tennis coach.

89. <u>Mario Marreiros</u>. Laundryman.

90. <u>Neil Berry</u>. From Sutton, Great London. Guest.

91. <u>Steve</u> and <u>Carolyn</u> Carpenter. Guests. Part of Gerry's more advanced tennis group.

92. <u>Jeremy "Jes" Wilkins</u>. Television Producer. Guest. Part of Ocean Club tennis group. Allegedly spoke to Gerry on the far side of Rua Dr Francisco Gentil Martins [the side of the road opposite the apartment]. His wife worked as a producer in the BBC crime unit. <u>Wilkins claimed he spoke to Gerry McCann right outside apartment 5A</u>, beside <u>the gate</u>.

93. <u>Rajinder Balu.</u> From Brentwood, Essex. Guest.

94. <u>Pamela Fenn</u>. [73] Guest. <u>Upstairs neighbor [5G] to the McCanns</u>. Claims she heard Madeleine crying for over an hour on the night of May 1st.

Notable Bloggers/Social Media Commentators

95. <u>Brenda Leyland</u>. [63] The owner of a Twitter account named @ sweepyface. She posted several critical tweets about Kate and Gerry McCann. She was found dead in March 2015, having apparently committed suicide.

Miscellaneous Support

96. <u>Pope Benedict XVI</u>. Blessed the McCanns at the Vatican in Rome, as well as an image of Madeleine on May 30th, 2007.

~

September 18ᵗʰ 2007

"Media was once about protecting a name; on the web it is about building one." — Ryan Holiday, Trust Me, I'm Lying: Confessions of a Media Manipulator

On a breezy blue but glassy clear September day in <u>Rothley, Leicestershire</u>, a gaggle of reporters gravitated towards an up-market home in one of the most affluent neighborhoods in Britain. They gathered outside on the sidewalk apparently as ordered.

Some in the group clutched notepads and pens beneath the September sun. Others were already aiming medium-sized lenses towards a wood and glass front door. And then, as if on cue, the front door of the large house opened.

The first to step out into the shaded exterior of the looming redbrick house had short grey hair and wore a pink shirt under a dark suit. In his left hand the man held a single sheet of paper with printed letters on both sides. He was followed out by a sombre looking couple; first a clean-shaven, neatly presentable man in his late thirties. The man, clearly younger than the man holding the sheet of paper, was dressed in navy blue trousers and a khaki green fleece.

Last out the door was a striking if slightly dour blonde. She was the one to close the front door. As the trio stepped forward in unison, the man in khaki took her hand and just as he did the woman in pink and white snuck a quick glance at the hovering media.

The walk across the driveway to the hovering cameramen and journalists was around 22 steps, taking the three in a gradual arc from the gloomy front door area to the sun-drenched sidewalk. As cameras whirred and pencils scratched, the couple almost immediately fell behind the tall man holding the sheet of paper. He seemed eager to meet the press right where they stood. There didn't seem to be a moment to lose.

The couple on the other hand soon allowed a gap of more than a metre to form, and part of the reason for this appeared to be the blonde woman, who – although linking hands with the man next to her – somehow took the widest and slowest route to get where they were going.

The tall man in the lead glanced over his shoulder, slowed and made a slight stomp of his foot, almost like a soldier non-verbally stamping the ground to "draw the line" between allies and foes.

The couple had hardly come to a standstill beside the man when he neatly slipped the note in his left hand to his right, stretched out his left arm in something of a flourish and warmly addressed the group huddled in front of him:

"*Morning. I'm Clarence Mitchell.*"

Someone had attempted to either respond to Mitchell's greeting, or the man beside him had also tried to say "morning." It was hard to say because Mitchell immediately launched into a prepared monologue.

The man in the pink shirt [which was unbuttoned at the top] identified himself further as the family's new spokesman. He added that he'd quit his career in government to assist the couple [who were both doctors]. He called them "innocent victims of a heinous crime."

Just as their spokesman said the words "innocent victims" the woman shot a glance at a cameraman beside her. Already her name, her husband's name and the name of their missing daughter – Madeleine McCann – were well known in Britain, Portugal and around the world.

Since Madeleine's disappearance on May 3rd almost six months earlier, the mainstream media and the British public had first sympathised with the couple, but then sympathy gave way to circumspection and finally suspicion.

"To suggest that they somehow harmed Madeleine, accidentally or otherwise[10]…[Mitchell glances down at his paper] is as ludicrous as it is nonsensical. Indeed, it would be laughable if it wasn't so serious. [Flips page without looking at it]. Because of the legal position that continues to exist in Portugal, I can't go into any further detail…"

Mitchell's golden voice conveyed the impression that the parents, Gerry and Kate McCann were both reasonable people who were both co-operating with the Portuguese authorities. In fact they had just left Portugal, almost immediately after the authorities there had labelled them "arguidos" [suspects].[11]

"The focus must now return to Madeleine and move away from the rampant, unfounded and inaccurate speculation of recent days. The focus

---

10 At the moment Mitchell paused after saying "they somehow harmed Madeleine, accidentally or otherwise…" Kate McCann shot a quick look at Mitchell then looked back down.

11 A government laboratory in Britain had conducted forensic tests indicating that DNA from Madeleine was in the trunk and beside the front passenger door of a rental car hired by the parents five weeks after her disappearance. The McCanns were labelled arguidos while in Praia da Luz, Portugal on September 7th, 2007. By September 9th they were back home in Rothley, Leicestershire.

must be the child at the very centre of all this: Madeleine. The task is simple: to find her and to understand why she has disappeared."

A black raven, unseen by the huddle of humans, flew over them, its wingbeats almost silent.

"Kate and Gerry are therefore again urging everyone to keep looking, not to forget the search for Madeleine, as they firmly believe that she could still be alive."

Mitchell spoke a few more words and had barely finished when the couple turned tail and headed back the way they'd come. Mitchell followed, evidently in a show of solidarity while adding that he'd be back shortly [presumably to answer questions].

Mitchell found himself behind the couple while Kate McCann – a regular jogger – took the inside lane and shortest route back. Mitchell quickly strode ahead and back into the shade where he ushered the couple back to their home, holding the door open for them like an untidy butler.

The couple stepped inside, having uttered not a single word, and the door then closed behind them. Mitchell then returned to the media to address their questions.

The Raven at the Edge of the World

*"Does wisdom perhaps appear on the earth as a
raven...inspired by the smell of carrion?"*
— Friedrich Nietzsche

A pile of human remains washes ashore beneath crooked limestone crags. The crags are incredibly far-flung, and the cadaver itself is somewhat held together by a disintegrating sack. Soon, vultures [Griffon and Egyptian] begin circling overhead as if each circle they make wills the flesh and bones to spill further out of the damaged hessian.

As the bleached and glistening limbs breach further into view, something very strange happens. A band of ravens appears and for reasons unknown, begin to guard the grotesquery from wild predators gathering in the air and on land. When the remains are discovered and re-buried elsewhere, so the legend goes, ten ravens continued their vigil.

From shakedowntitle.com:

*King Afonso Henriques (1139–1185) had the body of the saint exhumed in 1173 and brought it by ship to the Monastery of São Vicente de Fora in Lisbon, **still accompanied by the ravens.***

Looking at the ravens and vultures that haunt <u>the very same sea beaten site today</u> – known as Cape St. Vincent[12] – it's easy to imagine those events unfolding in the 4th century AD in the Roman province of Lusitania, happened mere moments ago.

In the same way, one little girl's disappearance ten years ago seems, in a sense, like it happened yesterday evening. In legal terms, nothing of substance has happened. A child lives one day and is gone the next. People are made suspects and then pardoned. There is a lot of chatter and a lot of sound and fury but in the end the child is gone and remains gone. The Madeleine McCann case is a ten-year-old unsolved mystery.

What if the whole world thought Madeleine McCann was missing when she was never abducted to begin with?

What if we turned to the ravens of Cape St. Vincent, and asked for assistance? For one to reconnoitre the coasts of the Algarve, for the flocks to comb the adjacent interior? What could come of hundreds of birds, like black daggers, cutting across the limestone landscape?

It is a question that really asks us to cut the cords that have tied us to this case, and to fly like balloons through natural maelstroms and see where these thermals mixed with intuitions lead. The raven is a totem for inspired thinking, but for that to happen it must be allowed out of the box. It must be allowed to fly wild and randomly, and perhaps it will return with a gift of some kind.

It may seem an unusual strategy, but we are not at home, we are in Portugal. When in Rome, do as the Romans do, when in Portugal, look to history. Look to the ravens. It's not a joke.

<u>The coat of arms of Lisbon</u>, Portugal's capital, depicts <u>two ravens on either side</u>. They are totems of wisdom and protection, and sometimes

---

12 It turned out those bones belonged to a Christian martyr – St. Vincent – and the shore where they washed up was named after him.

good fortune, perhaps because ravens have three particularly unusual traits: their longevity is exceptional, their intelligence at problem solving is unusual and their co-existence with humans runs through thousands of years of combined history.

The Vikings imagined the divine messengers of their god Odin as two ravens. Other Pacific borne cultures like the Inuits worshipped the raven itself as a god, sometimes as the Creator of the World, sometimes as a trickster god. In the Qur'an's version of Cain and Abel, a raven teaches Cain how to bury his murdered brother.

According to English legend, the Kingdom of England was supposed to fall if the ravens haunting the Tower of London were removed. That's the other thing about ravens; they're so successful in certain parts their flocks blacken the sky.

For some reason, the exposed crags of the most south-westerly point in mainland Europe has been a sanctuary of sorts for ravens and vultures. As such, the rugged Cape occupied by the ravens came to be seen as sacred ground. But not everyone saw it that way. The Greeks called the forbidding Cape the 'Land of the Serpents' while the Romans saw it as *Promontorium Sacrum*, a 'Holy Promontory'.

From shakedowntitle.com:

"For...terra firma-loving citizens of Rome, Cape St. Vincent was the 'Edge of the World', a supernatural vortex where the setting sun was dramatically submerged by the immense, unknown ocean...The [Edge of the World] myth persisted throughout the Middle Ages, until a man decided to end all that crazy nonsense and – in the process – put an end to the Age of Darkness..."

Truth, like beauty, is in the eye of the beholder. If we are to launch our search for the truth behind Madeleine's disappearance, I believe we should start here, about 30km from Praia da Luz. Staring out over the endless ocean there's a restless energy which speaks of possibilities deeper than we can fathom. The ocean knows many secrets and many graves.

On November 1st, 1755 at 09:40 the mighty Lisbon Earthquake shook the Algarve to its foundations, toppling towns from their perches into the sea and razing the capital of the Portuguese empire to the ground. In an instant, centuries of knowledge [nautical maps, calculations, records and charts] were buried beneath rubble and dust. Tsunamis washed hither and thither drowning 50 000 when Portugal's total population was less than 300 000. Portugal never recovered, and if anything, the Empire it held was ceded to others also using the sea to build their Empires.

Because the origin of the quake was 180km southwest of Cape St. Vincent, it was called St. Vincent's Fault.

From shakedowntitle.com:

"...in the vicinity where all the glory started to take shape, all the aspirations started to crumble. Yet, effulgent grandeur and abrupt changes of fortune were nothing new to the Cape. A real 'Playground of Empires', between 1337 and 1833 the watery surface off St. Vincent witnessed no less than nine major naval combats... this average number of almost two great military clashes per century accurately reflects the strategic importance of the Cape."

One can imagine on that otherwise quiet morning in November the ocean erupt, and with it, huge flocks of ravens. Just as Portuguese folk saw the sky turn black the Earth rumbled under their feet and their country crumbled before their eyes.

That was a long time ago but in a sense Portugal is still crumbling. The limestone appearance of the land, especially at the coast, gives it that crumbling aspect. The land itself resembles bleached bones and in fact, that's precisely what limestone is. By day the Algarve [Arabic for "The West"] burns bright, by night, it fades to pitch black.

Standing at the Cape today, the Portuguese Navy's St. Vincent Lighthouse on the southwestern edge of the Algarve is surrounded by a wall and closed to the public. Perched on the very edge of rugged, plunging limestone cliffs, the lighthouse is the second most powerful in Europe.[13] Its blinding beams shoot 60km across black oceans as it attempts to safeguard one of the world's busiest shipping lanes.

32km due East of the lighthouse, in other words well within range of its swooping searchlight,[14] is the jet black massif known as Rocha Negra [Black Rock] that looms over Praia da Luz, the tiny resort town where Madeleine fell off the edge of the world.

It is this volcanic rock that Kate McCann supposedly dreamt about, in mid-July 2007, as being the giant cradle of Madeleine's remains. This same hulk of Earth was invoked by a neighbour hours after Madeleine's disappearance. A car's headlights, it was claimed, had been seen moving somewhere along Rocha Negra's rough exterior.

At roughly the same time Kate dreamt of the Rocha Negra, Danie Krugel, a South African ex-cop was flown in. Based on the telemetry from his device [apparently able to track DNA over vast distances] Krugel also zeroed in on the hulking Black Rock.

Since the Rocha Negra is like an enormous blimp hovering over Praia da Luz, it seems to be the *most obvious place* where something [or someone] would be or could be missing for any length of time. For

---

13 The most powerful lighthouse in Europe is the Phare du Creach, in Brittanny, France.

14 The small jutting peninsula of Sagres obstructs the line of sight between Cape St. Vincent and Praia da Luz.

precisely that reason it's probably *the last place* anyone should look for Madeleine.

Instead we must look to the raven called *DOUBT*. It's sitting silently on the wall beside the towering lighthouse. A brisk breeze tugs at its glistening feathers. The creature's eyes seem to burn with a black fire. Its oily movements are sharp and fluid; other times slow and thoughtful. Then, abruptly it takes wing; a dagger cutting through swivelling beams of artificial light. The search for Madeleine has begun.

RAYS OF ARTIFICIAL LIGHT

"Is that all we have left? Is that all we are? Lights on a map that are slowly dying, hanging on for nothing?" — Carrie Ryan, The Dead-Tossed Waves

~

This is Madeleine

"I look back and think, why can't we just rewind the clock. And it takes you back to really happy memories, you know, and things you enjoyed. It's just a reminder of what isn't here anymore." — <u>Kate McCann to Oprah</u>,

The wings of the black bird beat the warm air. Its dark flight through the dark unknown is a search for <u>an almost four-year-old human child</u>.

<u>Madeleine was the oldest of three siblings</u>; <u>all three children the result of in-vitro fertilisation</u>.

According to her mother, <u>Madeleine was a "longed for" little girl</u> even before she was born. After getting married in Liverpool in December 1998, Kate and Gerry McCann immediately wanted children.

But sometimes life happens, or doesn't happen, while you're making other plans. Kate says, there was some disappointment attached to the "clinical requirement" of procreation when there was an intended biological result attached to it. Four and a half years after their weekend-before-Christmas wedding, when Kate and Gerry were both 35 years old, <u>Madeleine was finally born</u>.

The black wings beat on, a black bird leaning its flexible shoulders against the air current, borne back…

In Kate McCann's narrative, the chapter dealing with Madeleine [which comes after the chapter on Gerry] mostly deals with the attempts to conceive Madeleine, rather than Madeleine herself. At page eleven of fourteen Madeleine herself finally enters the narrative of her own chapter. It's all picture perfect. Kate's entire life revolves around "this little bundle" and Kate declares herself not to mind "in the slightest."

Kate also mentions the impact of baby Madeleine as "dramatic", and the surprise for herself and Gerry of "perfect" Madeleine "not being a little boy." Virtually in the same breath Madeleine's "200 decibel" scream is noted, with a relative exclaiming: "Jesus!" when she heard her crying over the phone. The semantics are worth noting. Kate doesn't say crying; instead Kate uses the word "screetch."

The first line of the next chapter begins with the words:

"Madeleine suffered from colic. She cried [most of the day]…" Much of the description around Madeleine centres not around happy memories, but – apparently – the arduous task of raising one child. The isolation. Kate describes the long days during the first six months and ongoing uncertainty on how to manage and care for the new arrival. When Gerry arrived home, Kate remarks, he was immediately handed Madeleine so that Kate could have her break.

The black wings work against the seam of night. Unzipping it, unearthing it, unburying what's hidden…

Perhaps most significant of all, Kate notes that Madeleine right from the get go "seemed to have an aversion to sleep." There's relief when Madeleine finally slept through the night, a full six hours when Madeleine was four months old. Significantly, this occurred while the family were attending a wedding in Italy. Kate is careful to note that Madeleine's ability to sleep soundly then was "for no obvious reason."

Kate also makes a point of noting that sleep wasn't a big deal for her, and yet the word "sleep" is mentioned 39 times in her book, "asleep" 17 times and "slept" 14 times. In sum the sleep theme is touched on a staggering 70 times.

When describing the first day of the holiday, Kate has Madeleine trip over the step of the airplane and score a large bruise on her shin. Kate uses the word "large", and is impressed that Madeleine doesn't cry despite the injury. From footage I've observed of Madeleine's fall, I find it difficult to believe she bruised herself at all with that stumble. It wasn't a hard fall, both children appeared to stay themselves with their hands and didn't have far to fall against the steps and besides all this, Madeleine was wearing socks beneath long trousers.

And yet Kate describes the edges of the steps as "sharp" and the bruise appearing "almost immediately."

There are several clinical descriptions in the McCann narrative that may suit the average doctor's diagnosis, but somehow seem out of place with a doctor-as-parent. Words like "compact" to describe Madeleine's body, and praising their daughter for "crying for ten seconds" as opposed to "the usual" ten minutes raises flags.

Black wings beating ceaselessly through the night…

During the early days following Madeleine's birth, we see Kate clearly predisposed to her friends. Kate mentions aimlessly walking about in town during the day while all her friends were at work [whereas her friends with children lived in Liverpool and Glasgow, not Leicester].

All of these seemingly trivial details would come to a head in the Algarve, in late April and early May 2007. A small community of families and their children decided to holiday together, and the setting for this holiday would become infamous forever after.

<u>Madeleine was a happy child</u>, so the story goes, outgoing…and her parents, doting…

It is into this maelstrom that the raven flies, its body dripping like drops of oil across shimmering stars of darkest night.

~

Ocean Club Orientation

"If you want to know what a man's like, take a good look at how he treats his inferiors, not his equals."
— Harry Potter and the Goblet of Fire

Like a black dagger the raven flies through beams of light – sunbeams, moonbeams, light beams, beams of time and tide – directly to a place called <u>Praia da Luz</u>. <u>After 30 kilometres</u> it swoops <u>over a conical hill</u> then drifts lower towards <u>a hodgepodge of gleaming apartment blocks</u> piled against each other like so many topsy turvy wedding cakes. Finally, with a flourish of black wings, the raven alights beside a yellow and blue sign that reads THE OCEAN CLUB and stands <u>under the shade of a tall Cyprus tree in Rua Dr. Francisco Gentil Martins</u>.

Next the raven flaps further down the drive and alights on a balcony across the road <u>directly opposite 5A</u>. From its perch the raven glances up and down the road and then, finding the coast clear, flaps down onto the warm tar surface.

<u>The big corvid waddles hurriedly</u> towards <u>apartment 5A. The kitchen area and living area both have windows facing the road</u>. Part of the patio area is also on the side of the road, connected to it by <u>a steep flight of narrow stairs</u> and secured by <u>a small gate</u> at <u>either end</u>.

The raven spots a man and a woman ambling down the road and so it flies further down the road alongside the boundary of the Ocean Club. The couple turn left off the downward sloping road and disappear into an alcove leading into the club, the Tapas bar, swimming pool and adjacent tennis courts.

Walking covertly, sometimes hopping, the raven heads back up the road carefully glancing left and right as it makes its way to the little gate plumb in front of and directly below 5A's first floor living room window. The black bird's gleaming beak points like an arrow towards the first floor window.

The light flickers suddenly, from day to night. Two men linger in the dark right beside the gate, under the living room window. [For the moment the raven ignores the Tanner sighting.]

And then in a black explosion of wings, the raven is gone.

~

Riddles in the Dark

"Photography helps people to see."
— Berenice Abbott

With the raven gone, what is there to guide us?

Is it a trick? To be brought here and left in the darkness to fend for ourselves? Aaah, says the raven, but you already have everything you need *right where you are*.

So, standing alone in the dark with looming, silent Cyprus trees for company in Rua Dr. Francisco Gentil Martins, what do we already have *right where we are*? Well, we have the physical infrastructure. We have the apartments clambering across night-time hillsides like mushrooms. We have gravity drawing us along a downward slope towards the warm waters of the North Atlantic.

And in our mind's eye, certainly, we have the "last photo" of Madeleine. The "last photo" was an exhibit showing a family man hanging out with his children, and also, that Madeleine herself appeared happy and healthy.

But, as you well know, appearances can be deceiving, which brings us back to the reason why we're here. We're here because Madeleine isn't. We're here because we're in the dark about what happened to Madeleine. We're here because even her parents maintain that though Madeleine is missing, she might even be alive and well. We're here because the riddles that began one dark night are still with us ten years later.

And what do we have ten years later? What is the last evidence of a living, breathing Madeleine? A photo drenched in sun. A little girl – her feet drenched in the icy water of the hotel pool.

The McCanns claim the photo of *a delighted and happy* Madeleine sitting with her feet in the pool beside her sister Amelie and her father at 14:29 on May 3rd, was taken hours before her "abduction."

What part of that claim is bogus, if any?

Just beyond the moon grey perimeter wall veiled by night is the swimming pool itself. This setting, black and cool by night, is where the "last photo" was taken. At night it is an oily eye, by day it is anything but – a blinding pearl of baby blue, flowing with spidery webs of dancing sunlight.

What part of that claim is bogus, if any? Well let's be clear about what the "last photo" claims:

1. *a delighted and happy Madeleine shortly before her disappearance*

2. *sitting with her feet in the pool*

3. *beside her sister Amelie and her father*

4. *at 14:29 on May 3rd*

5. *taken hours before her "abduction"*

6. *Madeleine was abducted*

Why would a conspiracy around the "last photo" even be necessary? Why did there need to be any fuss at all? The answer lies in the subject matter of the "last photo" itself. Why is it so important?

We see why the "last photo" is important by studying the potential counter claims the "last photo" appears to dispel:

1. That shortly before her death/disappearance Madeleine [and by extension the entire McCann clan] was not happy.
2. That Madeleine was not seen for a suspiciously long period before her disappearance [which could suggest the involvement of her parents].
3. That she wasn't part of a cohesive family.
4. That the photo was not taken either on the date or time claimed.
5. That mystery surrounds the hours before her "abduction" while Madeleine was in her mother's care.
6. That Madeleine was never abducted.

What if the purpose of the "last photo" was plausible deniability. Plausible deniability? For whom? For what? Well, perhaps for the cardiologist pictured in the image. Perhaps someone needed to hold onto their job at all costs.

Since Kate in the spring of 2007 was working part-time, Gerry was effectively the sole breadwinner for a family of five, and they'd just moved into an expensive new house. By April 2007, when the McCanns travelled to the Algarve, they'd been living in their new £500 000 detached home as a family of five for only a year.

Besides the new house and the surprise attached to Kate's second pregnancy [twins] I believe there are a few more symptoms that the McCanns were in a tight spot financially in April 2007.

Studying to become a doctor involves substantial costs. The British taxpayer foots a £610 000 bill for each doctor that it trains, while the doctor typically graduates into society shouldering a £70 000+ ball and chain in crushing student debt.

From shakedowntitle.com:

The average UK medical graduate is unlikely to ever fully repay large debts incurred whilst studying...A new analysis of salary data which looked at actual income of doctors, posed against record-high tuition fees and living costs, also showed that females were even less likely to ever be able to repay debts because they earn less per hour than male counterparts.... Their analysis of salaries for 4 286 medical graduates working more than 30 hours a week showed that the average doctor will have outstanding debts after 30 years...

The McCanns, in the more than decade-long run up to the events that eventually unfolded in the Algarve, were literally all over the place, working and living as far afield as New Zealand and Amsterdam, buying a home at one point only to rent it out the next while finding somewhere else in the world to live. Neither doctor though seemed on a clear-cut career course – the cardiologist ventured into sports physiology at one point, the GP from obstetrics and gynaecology [O & G] to neo-natal and back again.

Besides substantial costs, the training period involved is greater than most professions. It can take as long as ten years to transition from medical school graduation to consultant.

The time taken to get from medical school graduation to becoming a consultant varies from speciality to speciality but can be anything from seven to ten years. Gerry was appointed as a consultant cardiologist in Leicester [Glenfield Hospital] in 2005, the same year Madeleine's siblings, Amelie and Sean were born.

In theory, the McCanns combined debts in April 2007 would have been roughly £640 000 [their mortgage plus the combined student debt of two qualified doctors]. This amount doesn't take into account a previous "terraced" house jointly purchased by the couple, or the costs of Kate's in-vitro fertilisation [two successful courses but an unknown number that weren't over a five-year period] or indeed, any of the debt repaid over the two-year period since Gerry commenced work as a cardiologist at Glenfield.

Further potential evidence of financial malaise came via Gerry McCann's sister Patricia Cameron, in 2010.

From shakedowntitle.com:

*"When Madeleine first went missing, family and friends had to step in to **help them pay** the mortgage. **Money is constantly tight** but they have to keep going. They will never give up looking and that **costs money**. Families of the missing **still need to pay bills** while they search but there is no right to any **financial help**."*

In October 2007, three years prior to making these statements, the McCanns [who instead of returning to work remained in the Algarve for four months after Madeleine's disappearance] used the Find Madeleine Fund to make two mortgage payments.

Their spokesman Clarence Mitchell had to step forward to quell the outrage.

From shakedowntitle.com:

"The fund has always had the ability to assist the family financially if necessary. Kate and Gerry McCann stopped using the fund in September when they were made formal suspects in the case."

The Algarvian wind whispers through the roadside Cypresses, tugs at the poolside palm, swims across the slick eye of the pool, turning it into scales. The scales turn into a flurry of black feathers; the flock of ravens burst outward and scatter into the night.

The Devil in the Detail

"...that there was more to this world than meets the eye. Trees had spirits; the wind spoke. If you followed a toad or a raven deep into the heart of the forest, they were sure to lead you to something magical."
— Jennifer McMahon

Madeleine's disappearance is in many ways like peering into a black hole. There is no bottom, no end to it, and in the end, all the darkness does is reach outward into the darkness of the world, and the darkness in our own hearts.

Everything you need right where you are...

In a sense, we are faced with two possibilities. The innocent daylight, a little girl by a sparkling pool and no foul play, or the guilty night and a little girl stolen down a dark road. Which of these images is true?

Let's start by getting the obvious stuff out of the way. Is the "last photo" of Madeleine McCann taken eight hours before her death authentic? Either it is or it isn't. Some, like Richard, D. Hall, say no, it's not. I know what you're thinking. Easy to say, but how do you know?

As a professional photographer, I'm familiar with editing and metadata. Editing mischief can be traced through technical breadcrumbs or intuition. Using both to make our case for image chicanery is even better, so let's do that.

Now there are four main technical thrusts to the "last photo" debate. There's the vertical line controversy, the absence of shadows controversy, the proportions problem and the metadata controversy. Let's look at each of these and see how they stack up. What we're trying to determine though is whether the "last photo" of Madeleine McCann sitting beside her sister Amelie and her father Gerry, legs in the hotel pool, the scene splashed in sun, is in and of itself a fake.

1. Vertical Line Controversy

The reflection in Gerry's glasses [the right lens from the photographer's perspective] appears to have the swimming pool scene in the foreground turned on its side. Rather than seeing the side of the pool reflected as a horizontal line it's reflected vertically.

While admittedly it seems a little odd, what's clear is Gerry is sitting right beside a body of water and the other lens is clearly reflecting that, agreed? What's also clear is the right hand lens [from the photographer's perspective] is reflecting the right pool-edge section of the pool, even if it doesn't look – perhaps – quite the way we'd expect. Happy with that?

I'm not convinced there's any substance to the vertical substance controversy. You can view an "expert" assessment [though roughly put together] which includes a crudely practical demonstration of how a convex surface reflects its surroundings.

2. The Absence of Shadows Controversy

Shadows in photography led to one of the major arguments surrounding the moon-landing hoax. Compared to #1, this controversy is a lot tougher to call.

On the one hand, at face value Gerry and Amelie seem to be genuine enough, especially because of the shadow Amelie casts on Gerry's leg.

The tone and shape and shade of that would be very difficult to fake. The strange thing about the image is what seems to be the lack of shadow directly beneath Gerry's protruding elbow.

While I see the reasoning behind the argument, I'm not sure I buy it. Gerry's elbow is right behind Amelie's head, so any shadow cast would be almost directly below his elbow – vertically downward – so it could well be that the shadow is on Amelie's back or otherwise obscured by Amelie herself.

The white lounge chairs in the background are deceptive because the shadows appear to be stretching from left to right. This is a trick of the perspective because that end of the chair narrows as well.

Another trick is the apparent mismatch in shadows under Amelie's hat and Madeleine's. Again, while it looks a little off, I'm not sure whether it is. Madeleine's hat is a lot closer to her head, and the strand of her hair over her chest does cast the sort of shadow one would expect, and where one would expect.

I also don't buy the idea that Madeleine was added to the image after the fact because the tan wall behind her is fuzzy and out of focus. Some images do seem fuzzy and seem to have been photoshopped to support the argument. Others are crisp and so is the wall behind her, and so are all the edges of Madeleine herself.

The only minor complaints I have about this image are firstly the lack of shadow against the pool wall under Gerry's left leg [left from the photographer's perspective] and secondly that Madeleine as one of three subjects isn't connected to anyone else in the image narrative, either through her body, her shadows, through touching and perhaps most significantly, her demeanour.

While one can theoretically explain the lack of shadow as reflected light from the bottom of the pool, it does seem strange that on the blue mosaic directly below and behind Gerry's left knee there's no shadow, and no shading.

As for Madeleine, it may be that the coldness of the water is why she appears so thrilled. But why not show that delight to her mother right in front of her? If someone was calling her, at that moment, or if Madeleine noticed something in that moment, why do neither of her companions notice or respond to the same thing?

What's also apparent is all three people in the "last photo" have their attention directed somewhere else. There's very little cohesion, there's little syncing of the participants themselves and *none of the children take any notice of Kate* who supposedly took the photo.

In addition to this, note that the triangle of Gerry's elbow fits nicely into the indentation of Madeleine's hat. Just where his elbow juts out, Madeleine's white hat juts in. This sort of convenient *fitting in* on a photograph is sometimes a sign of editing interference.

I also don't like the fact that both children only show one arm prominently while the other almost looks amputated. It's harder to say whether this is a natural idiosyncrasy thanks to the angle of the subjects vis-a-vis the camera or whether the offending limbs have indeed been doctored out of sight.

Using edge analysis however, there doesn't seem to be any obvious problems, meaning either this is a genuine image or it was crafted by people who clearly knew what they were doing. I'm inclined to give the entire image a thumbs-up based on its face value, if nothing else.

3. The Proportions Problem

I guess there's a certain "it takes a thief to catch a thief" element to photography. Intuitively speaking, and as someone who has made regular use of swimming pools for numerous professional shoots, I can immediately feel that the bottom of the "last photo" image seems too tightly cropped. It's cropped too tightly and as a result there's a nasty and unnecessary amputation of the lower legs of all three subjects. Meanwhile the image unnecessarily indulges in the "dead space" above, which is filled with trees, pool chairs, the lawn, shade patterns and a creeper coloured wall.

One might argue that since the legs were dangling in the water, that there was no point in capturing that aspect of the image, but in fact the legs dangling in the water was *precisely why the picture was taken*. The natural place to crop the image would have been a sliver below where the legs are actually submerged in the pool, or even better, beneath the feet. Instead they're amputated at the knee and in Madeleine's case, even higher.

Look carefully and the theme of the image, *sitting in the pool*, is sidestepped entirely. Why? Because the water of the pool itself is missing. So the theme of the cropped image changes to: sitting ~~in the pool~~.

In a scenario where the family were at home and it was just another day, one might understand a willy-nilly focus from the photographer on *just capturing* three people. But in a scenario of a family holiday in an unusual location, with the focus being on fun, sun, swimming etc. [and Kate makes a big deal about Madeleine wanting to swim], then it makes no sense to exclude the key highlight of the image – the swimming pool. The sensible way to take the photo would be to have your subjects in the centre and equal parts water in the foreground and air space above the head.

This might be over-analysing, especially since Kate McCann wasn't trying to win an award for her photography, but an apparently trivial detail like how the final family photo was cropped matters when we know that *Madeleine had a large bruise on her leg*. How would a "last photo" look, especially where her parents might be suspected of neglect or worse, if Madeleine was sporting a bruise? Well, it wouldn't do, would it?

4. Metadata Controversy

Professional photographers work a fair amount with metadata. I do my own copyrighted covers for Kindle which means saving my name and the book's name into the Metadata to, for example, make it more searchable.

Metadata on a photo is broadly analogous to data properties on a common computer file. Right click on a file [say a Word.doc] and you can examine its properties at a single glance: date, time, size, modifications, permissions and various other settings. The main difference is that the computer automatically assigns these file properties. The user typically can't change much besides the name of the file. To alter dates and times and file sizes requires re-saving the file and having the computer re-assign new values.

Metadata on images has these items too but tends to be more involved, noting ISO values, aperture settings, shutter speed, equipment used etc. Many of these details are useful references when either trying to fine-tune photos in the field or noting the settings of a perfect shot to oneself or others [for example in travel and photography magazines].

When submitting photographic material to be sold as stock images, the metadata is a real bitch to worth with and can suck up a lot of time. Captions are typically included in stock metadata. Magazine picture editors will also examine metadata to determine, for example, whether a borderline image meets prescribed minimum standards. Photographic assignments can also involve mandatory settings, and any issues with quality tend to be debated by citing the metadata.

Metadata in crime scene photographs are useful in the recording of the chronology of photos, <u>as occurred in the Oscar Pistorius trial</u>.[15]

Where the "last photo" controversy gains traction, as far as I'm concerned, isn't in the manipulating of what's in the photo or down to any explicit photo editing technique, but rather in the "last photo" *narrative*. The metadata seems to play directly into that and not insignificantly.

---

15 From shakedowntitle.com: *"Let me assist you with your timeline,"* Roux *said, reminding him that he had arrived on the scene at 5.12am. He said he had followed all the photographs with the metadata and was able to follow step-by-step how Van Staden had moved through the scene and at what time he had been at each point. At 5.23am, Roux said, Van Staden had taken photographs of Reeva Steenkamp lying at the bottom of the stairs. Roux then commented that Van Staden hadn't filed all his photographs chronologically and that his numbering was "strange" as they appeared out of sequence with his timeline...*

Fiddling with ~~Metadata~~ Four and Twenty Blackbirds

"The trust of the innocent is the liar's most useful tool." — Stephen King

Fiddling with Metadata is, if you'll pardon the pun, child's play. The whole point of a photograph's metadata is that one goes in and fiddles with it, whether to rename or manually catalogue a photo, to caption it, for search engine optimisation or…well, to *malinger*.

The asterisk at the end of the last chapter illustrates just how metadata can be used to re-frame a narrative, where the metadata is actually seen as a sort of inviolable source code, similar to cell phone data. By mischievously fudging the data and then holding it up as inviolable source code, it can do a lot to impinge on the credibility of a hostile witness.

The McCann metadata is allegory for a well-known English nursery rhyme.

Sing a song of sixpence, A pocket full of rye. Four and twenty blackbirds, Baked in a pie.

The blackbirds are not blackbirds at all, but symbols of *the hours in the day*. The origins are said to come from Shakespeare's *Twelfth Night*, and the idea of singing a song comes from this:

"Come on; there is sixpence for you: let's have a song."

In other words, the particular song with a particular rhyme and rhythm has financial incentives attached. It's not sing a song of sixpence but *for* sixpence. What more than that?

Well, it appears to be more than just a song, it's a coded message. See if you can decipher the metadata in the remainder of the nursery rhyme:

The birds began to sing; Wasn't that a dainty dish, To set before the king. The king was in his counting house, Counting out his money; The queen was in the parlour, Eating bread and honey. The maid was in the garden, Hanging out the clothes, When down came a blackbird, And pecked off her nose.

The king, in some interpretations, symbolises the sun, the queen the moon and the blackbirds as hours, sometimes as monks. In other traditions, where the rhyme was related to the Reformation and the printing of the original English Bible, the blackbird represents letters of the alphabet. The pecking off of the maid's nose is seen as *a demon stealing her soul.*

The allegory of the rhyme is conjured yet again when the context shifts to transformations between 1536 and 1541 in Britain. Henry VIII disbanded the Catholic Church and disposed of their assets.

Counting out his money...

During the "Suppression of the Monasteries" Anne Boleyn [the maid] became the King's wife, while the Queen, Catherine of Aragon was divorced, deposed and banished from the court. The rhyme as political verse seems to attest to a folkloristic sympathy with the Queen by having the Maid cursed, and her nose pecked off.

The rearranging of metadata of the "last photo" is really about baking four and twenty blackbirds into a pie in order to hold onto six pence. Later, the singing of a particular song earns the McCanns a pocket full of rye.

Baking twenty-four blackbirds into a pie is really about one thing: *changing time.*

~

ETA from Faro Airport

"Fantasy is unconstrained by truth."
— Hilary Mantel, Wolf Hall

From the moment the McCanns touch down in the Algarve, time seems to become soapy and slippery. Kate provides absolutely no details regarding time of arrival at Faro airport 90.2km due East of Praia da Luz, or at the Ocean Club itself on April 28th, 2007.

However, we know from Gerry McCann's statement to Portuguese police on May 10th, 2007 that:

1. The McCanns arrived at Faro in Portugal from East Midlands Airport at 12:30.

2. They "immediately" travelled to Ocean Club via the airport mini-bus, arriving at the hotel two hours later at 14:20/14:30.

3. According to Gerry check-in took half an hour, taking the clock to 15:00 in the afternoon.

4. Unpacking in apartment 5A went on until 16:45.

5. The whole group, including children, arrived in the Tapas area at around 17:00.

At this point [point number 5 at 17:00] a "pool" is mentioned for the first time in Gerry's statement.

On so simple a matter as their arrival as a family in Praia da Luz Gerry and Kate can't seem to agree. Kate has the family seamlessly leaving Faro airport [the carrier – British Midland International – is not mentioned either] and arriving at the Ocean Club half an hour later than Gerry does. Perhaps Kate's 15:00 timestamp errs a little on the late side in her book published four years after the fact. If so, so what?

Well, Gerry's statement to police two weeks after Madeleine vanished has check-in of a large group at hotel reception at the Ocean Club *completed* by 15:00. So it seems there's already a 30-40 minute discrepancy just on the simple point of their time of arrival at the hotel. And then there's a third timestamp. The lead investigator Goncalo Amaral has the McCanns touching down at the airport at "around 14:00", while the Oldfields and O'Briens had arrived at 13:00.[16]

Now, according to Kate, at the airport they found their pre-booked "people carrier" and driver [odd terms for a mini-bus, but easy to confuse with airline carrier]. The "pre-booking" is certainly indicative of a fairly smooth and rapid transition through the airport. But no matter whose ETA we accept, the point is by the time the McCanns arrived, transport had already been arranged for their group by the first group to arrive. This would have expedited their transit tremendously. We can also say with some certainty that if a group arrived earlier than the McCanns, waiting patiently for their arrival would mean that by the time the McCanns [and company] did arrive, there'd be less dilly-dallying than if it was the other way round.

Since the transit was around one hour, how likely is it that the McCanns dawdled at Faro airport – arriving in the off season – for an additional hour or more?

---

16 Source: *The Truth of the Lie.*

Faro airport was enlarged in 2001, and in 2007 44.8% of the entire tourist trade to the Algarve was from British tourists. Three of the five most frequent airlines into the Algarve were from British airlines. In June alone, <u>Faro handled 2599 flights and almost 400 000 British passengers</u> hailing from airports in London, Manchester and Birmingham. And this was only half the total tourist load Faro had to process.

We can safely assume, therefore, that in April 2007, when Faro was significantly quieter, processing and transit through the airport, especially for British travellers who were in the majority, would have been speedy.

So, it's possible we have a half hour or an hour on day one in the Algarve that's not fully accounted for. Given that the digital display of the last photo read 13:29 [exactly an hour after touchdown, and given a 55-minute estimated travel time from Faro to Luz, it's possible that the "last photo" was actually the "first photo."

Baking twenty-four blackbirds into a pie is really about one thing: *changing time.*

But how could that be?

Well it could be if someone else besides the McCanns booked the group into reception, the McCanns could have changed and hung out at the pool until the admin was sorted. They did, after all, have the most children of the group although not the youngest. Another possibility is that Kate took care of booking in the family while Gerry and the kids hung out at the pool.

Do you see where we are? We're back at the pool, back at the last photo.

In her book, Kate mentions Madeleine insisting on going for a swim in the "freezing" swimming pool *immediately after arriving at the resort.*

Kate isn't in the mood, because she feels the cold and a cool breeze was blowing.

Not only does Madeleine swim but Kate does too and this is witnessed by an anonymous man sitting poolside with his two sons. Kate is very clear to say the man was watching them while they swam. Kate also acknowledges the man by saying to him, "The things you do for your children…" a reference it seems to the torture of swimming with Madeleine.

According to Kate the water was so cold they were still shivering three hours later. The problem is, Kate's story and Gerry's statement don't jibe, and they need to, because Gerry is *in* Kate's photo.

Ultimately though, does *any* of this really matter? If so, *why* does it matter?

If the "last photo" is not the last photo after all, then a large hole erupts into the timeline of Madeleine's disappearance on May 3rd. Not only that, but other questions emerge too. Such as: how happy was Madeleine on the day she disappeared? And did her unhappiness play into her disappearance at all?

There's also another serious problem with a scenario where the "last photo" is actually the first [or a much earlier] photo. Consider the obvious. If *not many photos of Madeleine* had been taken during a week-long family holiday, this *alone* would arouse suspicion.

In the Justin Ross Harris case, where Harris' two-year-old son Cooper was left to die in Harris' SUV, it was found in court that Harris stopped taking photos of Cooper two weeks before his son's death. This was specifically noted and raised by Cooper's day-care teacher to Harris directly. Harris' response was that Cooper [just two years old at the time] was getting older. WTF!

We also see a parallel in the Ramsey case, where *very few photos* were taken on that particular Christmas. So much so that in many documentaries, other Christmas footage is mined and used as a proxy for JonBenét's last Christmas. Sinister, isn't it?

One might ask why parents would purposefully get rid of photographic evidence [if they did at all]. Well the reasons are obvious. Clothing worn by the victim, and also worn by those accompanying them in photographs, would clearly show investigators what sort of fibres to look out for. Demeanour and superficial injuries [Madeleine had a large bruise on her leg] would also be useful to probe potential underlying emotions and possible discord.

More troubling, if there was no photo to corroborate Madeleine's whereabouts at around 14:30 on May 3rd, the date of her abduction, then there was very little else to account not only for her movements that afternoon, but also her wellbeing. Take away the 14:30 photograph and the inevitable – and dreadful – question arises:

Was Madeleine still alive at 14:30?

Kate's book, written in 2011, very clearly "corroborates" the idea that the pool photo was the last photo, and very clearly timestamps it as just prior to 14:40 [even though the camera display read 13:29]. This timestamping is quite specific from Kate given how unspecific other details are, like arriving at and leaving the airport on Saturday April 28th. It should also be noted that Britain and Portugal are on the same time zone.

Kate is absolutely clear to emphasize:

"I took what was has turned out to be <u>the last photograph to date of Madeleine</u>."

But there's a clear problem with Kate's version of events here.

Since Gerry is *in* the actual photo, why does Gerry fail to mention *anything* about the swimming pool in his statement to police regarding their movements on the day of their arrival?

The swimming pool is mentioned once around the 17:00 timestamp, but with no mention of swimming or photos. If Gerry wanted to establish and confirm his movements, wouldn't it make sense to refer to photos and to use them to say, "See, here's the photo showing what I said I was doing…"

But he doesn't.

Which brings us at last to the moment of truth wherein the anomaly – the photograph – is revealed as both beginning *and* end.

~

Nothing like the Sun

"My mistress' eyes are nothing like the sun."
— Shakespeare's Sonnet No. 130

"At the end of April 2007, it's spring in the Algarve,
even if the weather is particularly gloomy. It rains
often. While the sun shines, the temperature becomes
pleasant, but the nights are cold and windy."
— Goncalo Amaral, The Truth of the Lie

A front of clouds moves across the starry sky, blanketing the night over the Ocean Club in an oppressive darkness. If there are any ravens here, now, they are entirely invisible. All there is left to do then is wait for the dawn. Since it's not even midnight, and cold and windy, it's going to be a long wait.

If <u>the problem in this case is time</u>, it's also the solution. What happens when you rearrange chronology? Well, you must fit the dislodged puzzle piece [like the "last photo"] into a *different* time. The question is how does it fit?

The McCanns demonstrate their storytelling sophistication – I think – through their mirroring technique in their narrative. Oscar Pistorius did something similar, by conjuring a scenario which mirrored the actual events when he shot Reeva Steenkamp, yet also opened the door to a phantom scenario.

Theoretically the photo *can* fit at either end. The photograph is revealed as both a picture of the beginning of the holiday and the end.

But, in reality, of course, the photo was only taken once. So, when was it taken? In true crime *proving* a misdirection tends to be difficult, because misdirections float on bubbling seas of uncertainty.

Not so in this case. The misdirection is fairly straightforward.

In *BBC's Panorama* film broadcast on November 19, 2007 <u>Kate's mother Susan Healy describes a call home</u>:

"[Kate] said it was cold. That the weather was cold and they were quite surprised because they hadn't taken a lot of warm clothing. Uhm... and so, she was surprised about that. But I think the day I was speaking to her it had improved a bit. And I think she said that they were going down to the beach."

There's a lot to mine from Healy's comments. Firstly, it's abundantly clear that it was cold – not cool – cold. Remember, these are folks from upper England and Scotland, so especially to them, cold is a relative term. In terms of the Algarve then [visited in the spring off-season], it wasn't *quite* the right time to be there. So, why were they? Well, it was cheaper.

Something else Healy emphasises is Kate's "surprise". She mentions it twice and notice the word she uses. Surprise is a neutral word. Disappointment would have been more apt. Imagine going on a beach holiday but finding the weather too cold, dreary and unpleasant for the beach, or for swimming? Think about what that means. You've left rainy England for a break, a break in the long winter but also – perhaps – a break from the children. If the weather is cold, then what sort of break is it going to be? If anything, cold weather is going to sort of keep the family huddled together in the confines of a new, temporary home, and with that must come the frustration of paying to be somewhere but also being stuck because of the weather.

What's also interesting from Healy is the failure to say exactly when the weather had improved. By qualifying that the weather had improved "a bit" and that she thought Kate said they were going to the beach – rather than that they most certainly were – points to a lack of conviction.

And weather records clearly show Healy's doubtfulness is justified. The weather during their week-long stay clearly deteriorated from the first day [Saturday April 28th] until the day of Madeleine's disappearance [Thursday May 3rd].

Maximum temperatures steadily declined from 22 °C on their first day in the Algarve to 19 °C on May 3rd. [The average maximum temperature for that time of year was 22 °C]. Minimum temperatures were below average on day one at 11 °C, 10 °C on day two but rose gradually to 13 °C on May 3rd [but was still below the average 14 °C minimum for that time of year]. In other words, it was a slightly cooler season there and then in 2007.

In the Ramsey case, the Christmas of 1996 was also unusually cold compared to other days of the same month, and the same day compared over various years. The impact of the weather on families is quite simple – it keeps them together and while on holiday, has a sort of cheek by jowl effect.

In Kate's narrative, the word "beach" is referenced 29 times, but on only one occasion do the McCanns actually head to the beach as a family. This happened on the afternoon of Tuesday the 1st of May, their third day on holiday, so basically the halfway mark in their family vacation.

While Kate talks about "just the five of us" doing something together for a change, she also notes that "to be honest", the kids would probably have been happier in their creche's. I think this says a lot about Kate, how Kate appraises her children and possibly how the kids felt about being with their parents.

Kate acknowledges the "weather wasn't great" for their special outing together, and once on the beach that "it started to rain." Kate also regretfully sums up the activity with a hint of bitterness, describing it as "not exactly a roaring success."

I'm not sure the family holiday was either. Think about it; is there a *single photo* of Madeleine on the beach? Are there any group family photos that clearly show a family having fun and having a genuine break from the sterile routines in Rothley?

Kate's invoking of rain cuts to the heart of the McCann narrative. It rained on their parade in the Algarve, and Madeleine's death was the climax to a grey and stormy week. It's when we picture the holiday as it probably was – more drab than bright – we see why the "last photo" is so important, and also where the extent of the misdirection is made manifest.

Now weather records for Faro approximately 100km due East of their location describe the cloud cover on May 1st, 2007 as "mostly cloudy". The temperature in the afternoon was a miserable 17.0 °C and this was exacerbated by wind chill, with gusts blowing in at 25.9 km/h / 7.2 m/s and rising as the afternoon went on. Of all the days the McCanns chose to go to the beach, this one was one of the worst. The morning was clearer, but also cold and draughty. Since these temperatures are based on Faro airport, which would have some wind protection, it's possible the McCanns experienced even colder and windier conditions in Praia da Luz than the available record shows. Clearly the Faro weather centre doesn't indicate any precipitation for May 1st.

A strange sound like the jingle of metal can be heard in the dark. Squinting towards it, up, it takes a moment to make out the gleam in the dark. A raven sits on the perimeter fence around the tennis court. Its silhouette seems to melt into the black night behind it. But a glint of light from its beak beckons toward the twin dark squares of the courts. More glints indicate the blinking from small, black, all-seeing eyes.

What does the raven wish us to see at the tennis court?

The raven croaks, almost like the bark of a dog, into the dead silent, coal black night.

Madeleine, of course

Kate's narrative has the family heading to the beach on the same day another photograph was taken of Madeleine, the "tennis balls photo." Knowing what we know about May 1st, Madeleine in shorts is under-dressed for the weather. We can also clearly see from the light quality that the sun isn't shining. It wasn't the first time either.

Referring to May 3rd [two days later], Kate says it was on "the cool side." Remember the word Susan Healy used, quoting Kate: "cold". That's probably the word Kate did use, and Kate goes on in her narrative to describe herself as thin skinned when it came to cold weather. When describing Sunday night [April 29th] at the Tapas bar, Kate wears five layers of clothing because it was "very cold and windy".

But when it comes to the storytelling around May 3rd, the day of Madeleine's "abduction", a euphemism is employed. It was "cool" enough for Kate to note she wished she'd brought a cardigan for Madeleine so she wouldn't get cold. No big deal, right?

Well it is a big deal: if it was too cool to go to the beach it was too cool to sit by the pool. If it was too cool to sit by the pool, then why does the "last photo" look like it was a perfect summer day?

Interestingly immediately after Madeleine's disappearance, Kate's first worry was that her daughter might be cold. Juxtaposed right beside "Madeleine! Madeleine!" Kate has the words "cold and windy". A few lines earlier she describes running out into the chill to alert the Tapas Seven. Kate describes their reaction as "frozen" and then, even more presciently, Kate sees Madeleine in her Eeyore top [which she'd washed earlier that day] and "feels how chilled" Madeleine is/would be.

Shortly after the narrator offers a medical diagnosis: that Madeleine might have been dumped somewhere and that she was "dying of hypothermia." This is a coded way of saying that she worried that cold weather, or the elements rather than her abductor, may have already claimed her life.

Let's be explicit: this is also a psychological nod to the Justin Ross Harris case, where Harris doesn't kill his two-year-old son, Cooper, and he's not responsible for what happens to the little boy. The car he's left in does the killing; it's the car's fault. The sun kills Cooper. It's the sun's fault. Little Cooper dies not of hypothermia but the opposite – hyperthermia [death by overheating].

In the JonBenét Ramsey case John Ramsey doesn't conduct much of a search of his own home [his daughter JonBenét lies dead in the family basement for around seven hours, with the police, family and family friends present] but what he does do is look inside a walk-in refrigerator. He wonders:

"Could JonBenét have been put inside, trapped there?"

JonBenét was placed inside a small room in the basement, and the door secured from the outside. Since it was mid-winter and the room was bare, and JonBenét was on the floor, it was much like being placed inside a cold refrigerator.

During the police interrogation in June 1998 John Ramsey said of his daughter's disappearance:

*"I think I ran back up and looked in her room, and I think accepted the fact that she was gone. And you know, I don't remember, I mean I said I remember I looked in the refrigerator. Just – I just tried to look in places like – (INAUDIBLE). I wasn't looking for her hiding. That wasn't in the equation, but, I – I, I think I just accepted that she was gone from the house pretty quick. As did I think the police. Of course, we used to operate on that assumption that **I was worried about her being cold**, you know, it was wintertime. All these thoughts go through your head."*

This is psychological mirroring of a narrative; it is a subconscious symbolism of what the storyteller wants to say in circumstances where he or she perhaps feels forbidden from being completely forthright.

The raven skittles the chain-link fence.

Madeleine, of course

The photograph of Madeleine on the tennis court *also* appears to be doctored. The original is clearly taken on a cold and dreary day. Doctored images are both cropped and brightened. Think about the message the undoctored photo actually sends. A little girl who looks entirely alone on a large, bare, shadowy court. It's not a happy picture at all. Madeleine's expression, though she's smiling, suggests to me that she was recently crying. It's in her eyes. There's a puffiness about them, and something forced about the poor little girl's smile that looks more miserable than it does joyous.

There's video where Kate and Gerry prompt Madeleine to smile, but just as quickly the smile vanishes.

People who smile are described as sunny or as sunshine. By the same token, sadness, dysfunction and depression is seen as dark, shadowy and a nightmare. The symbolism of cold [as death] and cloudiness [for a dysfunctional family] may seem entirely theoretical, until we examine the actual photographs and weather records.

The "last photo" recorded at 14:29 [or 13:29 according to its display] is nevertheless anchored to the weather history. In the photo, it is sunny and apparently warm. The weather on May 3rd at midday was relatively cool 17-19 °C [about 66.20 °C] <u>based on weather records</u>. I don't know about you, but 17°C even as water temperature is brisk, never mind as ambient temperature. Perhaps more important, it was by no means a sunny day on May 3rd. The weather report clearly indicates cloudy conditions for midday and the afternoon on May 3rd.

April 28th on the other hand was forecast as "clear" [i.e. sunny] until 15:00. The wind rose from a fairly calm 16.7 km/h / 4.6 m/s at 13:00 to almost twice the wind speed – 27.8 km/h / 7.7 m/s – half an hour later. By 14:30 it was an umbrella crunching gust[17] billowing at 33.3 km/h.

The following day was even clearer but by 11:30 far gustier [as Kate confirms], with the wind blasting West South West between 29.6 km/h / 8.2 m/s and 31.5 km/h / 8.7 m/s between 13:00 and 14:30. At times it powered up to 39 km/h, approaching the lower end of gale force.

April 30th was both cloudier, windier [at 41km/h] and colder. May 1st saw the winds die down somewhat [37km/h], but it was a chilly day with cloud and rain from midday onwards. May 2nd was also much the same as May 1st – wind, cloud, cold and rain between 01:00 and 11:00. May 3rd saw the wind die down but the day remained cold and cloudy.

Returning to Kate's version of events between 13:30 and 14:30 on May 3rd, 2007, imagine a cool, overcast day with a slight breeze. Kate places Dr. Fiona Payne in a scene close to midday where Madeleine is walking in front of both of them swinging her arms. When Fiona

17 According to the Beaufort scale a gale is defined as a wind blowing 50-102 km/h.

exits for lunch, the entire McCann family do the same – returning to their apartment 5A straddling Rua Dr Agostinho da Silva for their lunch. Kate had already prepared lunch, and washed a large stain on Madeleine's Eeyore top. The family arrived home, ate and then…what?

Strange, the McCanns' last sit down meal together as a family isn't even mentioned. Amanda Knox does the same thing when writing about her last meal with Meredith Kercher in the villa [by the same time the next day Kercher was dead]. The Ramseys are also coy about details of their last meal as a family in their account.

In the case of the McCanns, nothing that was said or done, or eaten, is shared. Instead, Kate reveals that the children were getting "quite restless" in the apartment. So, what did the family do? The family headed out, despite the cool weather [and still no cardigan for Madeleine] they ended up sitting around and dipping their feet in the toddler pool. Because that's where you go when it's cold and cloudy – to the pool.

I have seen other research into the "last photo" debacle, and a popular view is that it was taken on April 29th. The sunshine on that day makes it a good candidate,[18] but not the wind. Kate McCann's narrative is fairly muddy for the period midday to the afternoon on April 29th, so it's not entirely out of the realm of probability.

I realise the timeline is tight from the airport to the swimming pool, but in a sense, if the display clock is right, the photo was taken at the first possible moment the McCanns arrived. This seems likely. As children,

---

18 There are additional reasons why April 29th is a possible candidate day for the "last photo." The "pool area" background of this image indicates it was definitely taken during the family holiday. The clothing appears to match what Madeleine wore onto the plane when they departed the East Midlands Airport. The crinkled jeans in the knee area may attest to Madeleine's stumble against the runway stair. Note the overcast conditions.

we always made a beeline to the sea after interminable months lived inland in hot, dry South Africa.

I have three additional reasons for picking April 28th as the date of the last photo. Two have to do with Gerry, and one with Madeleine herself.

The raven rattles the cage; cackles. It is completely invisible in the dark, and yet it's definitely there; moving, lurking, beckoning.

1. If Madeleine *had* bruised her leg on April 28th, it might have been suggested by one of the doctors in the retinue[19] [or her doctor-parents] that cold water be used to "treat" the injury. It's clear from the "last photo" that Madeleine hasn't arrived at the pool to swim, she's not wearing a costume and no towels are in sight. Neither, for that matter, has anyone else.

   If the photo was taken *on the first day at the hotel* in the Algarve rather than the last, there would be a bruise and in terms of using the photo for publicity, there would be *cause* to tightly crop the image to hide that bruise.[20]

2. Gerry McCann's off-white t-shirt appears to be the same shirt worn in the transit bus on the day the family arrived in the

---

19 At the core of the Tapas Seven were four doctors as well as Diane Webster, Dr. Payne's mother in law. Including the McCanns, the Tapas Nine were a cabal of six doctors, a doctor's wife [Rachael Mampilly], a doctor's partner [Tanner] and Webster, all of whom had cause to be motivated by family allegiance.

20 The "tennis balls photo" shows a right side profile of Madeleine, from Madeleine's perspective. If the bruise was on the inside of Madeleine's lower left leg or the outside of the right shin, in other words the reverse angle to the "tennis balls photo", then a brightly lit uncropped "last photo" of Madeleine wearing shorts would have revealed it.

Algarve. If it is the same shirt, then #3 emerges as a distinct possibility.

3. The sweat on Gerry's forehead in the pool image may not be due to the warm weather but the result of lugging the family's airplane luggage around earlier that day. Notice, also, what's missing [or obscured] between the video and the pool image – Gerry's watch.

If the problem is time, the timeline is also where the answers to this deeply layered case lie hidden. And with that knowledge there's a faint beating of black wings in the night. Once more the black bird has taken flight.

~

Countdown to a Disappearing Act

"Raven is a priestess at Avalon by the time Morgaine arrives… Since she has taken a vow of silence, very few ever hear her speak." — Marion Zimmer Bradley, The Mists of Avalon

Once the raven has disappeared into the darkness, it is as though the abyss of the black night deepens even further, and its wet maw opens and closes at one's feet. Abruptly one is no longer at the Ocean Club but somewhere else. Well, it's not quite that one is somewhere else, just that one is no longer *above ground*.

But how can this be?

A rough, irregular ceiling built by Roman hands feels close to the sunken head and bent shoulders. Wherever this is, it feels – or sounds – closer to the sea. Salty foam hisses and sucks over sand and rock. There's an impatient call. The sound of the black bird barely breaks through the murmur and wash of waves.

Moving towards it the waves and the raven's call grows louder.

From shakedowntitle.com:

…the Ocean Club resort in Praia da Luz, where the McCanns stayed, was built around Roman ruins that were part of a small fishing settlement in the third to fifth centuries.

There is also *a Roman burial site and ruins* include an aqueduct, wells, fish salting tanks, the remains of a Roman bathhouse and at least eight *tunnels*....

One is drawn through the subterranean darkness as if by nothing more tangible than gravity and sound, and with every passing moment and every passing metre [and there are around seventy metres of tunnel] the hissing of water becomes more urgent, the raucous caw of the raven more jarring. And then a circle in the dark opens up to reveal the faint lines of a humble medieval tower. Set against the crawling Atlantic is the barely discernible Church of Nossa Senhora da Luz ['Our Lady of Light'] built in 1521.

Much of what went into our Lady was destroyed by the Lisbon Quake [well, whatever happened 200 odd kilometres off Cape St. Vincent in 1770-something]. The surviving superstructure [above and below ground] was further damaged by a violent storm and a second earthquake in 1969.

But the Lady remained in some shape or form, above and below the ground, so that there developed a sort of tussle by congregants between members of the Portuguese Roman Catholic Church and the Church of England. Today [and tonight] the church belongs to both.

Madeleine, of course

Standing in front of the rather squat building, there's very little sense of its history. So much has been reconstructed here that whatever once lay beneath is somehow…hard to recognise. The raven sits above the doorway, above a round, porthole-like window, perched on a wrought iron crucifix. It moves impatiently on its perch, its beak darting towards a rooster at the very top of the tower. The rooster is a wind-vane, and the wind nags urgently at-. Or no, the black beak dabs lower…not at the wind vane but at the clock.

Set into a steeple, steeped in darkness, the black hands don't seem to point anywhere.

The raven cocks its head. Its fiery black eyes blink.

Oh, but they do

Madeleine, of course

In the previous chapter, we found out about the deteriorating weather patterns. We saw that by May 3rd, the weather was just starting to turn, however it was nothing like a sunny day. The aftermath, however would be both warm and sunny, a strange irony given the pall that was hanging over Praia da Luz, and this lady, that morning.

And so, to the clock… What does it tell us? It tells of the schedule [more so from the 29th of April onwards than the 28th] and of the timekeeping that leads into the timeline itself. Its rusted gears and levers turn and grind down to the mincemeat of the actual Disappearing Act.

April 28th

- Breakfast at the airport in England.
- Madeleine bruises leg, whimpers, but doesn't cry. Kate describes Madeleine as "brave", "behaving perfectly" and forgetting about her sore leg. Kate also forgets about the leg as there are no further references to it, including treating the injury.
- Transit. Some commentators believe <u>Gerry McCann, while sitting glumly on the far side of a row of small children</u> on the airport bus says:[21]

---

21 <u>Kate McCann is on the other side of the rear seat of the airport bus.</u>

"Fuck off. I'm not here to enjoy myself."

- The McCanns move into ~~an upmarket~~ a middle-class-ish ground floor apartment. Unlike David and Fiona's apartment, the McCann's apartment 5A has no sea view.

- Kate notes that the benefit of the ground floor was not having to worry about children's safety on the balcony. This is a telling comment, both because it suggests they didn't wish to worry and also because in fact they did: a dangerously steep staircase led directly from the porch at 5A. The sheer wall framing both sides of the narrow staircase was also too high for a child of three, almost four, to have a hope of staying a stumble or gaining any purchase during a serious fall.

- The McCanns have left their "double-buggy" child carrier in Leicestershire. This means their small children [Sean and Amelie at two-years and three-months, and Madeleine at three-years and eleven-months[22]] have to be carried over longer distances.

- According to Kate, they barely used the front door, instead coming and going each day up and down the same steep stairway. Bear in mind Madeleine's stumble on the small stairs leading to the plane when they departed England and imagine the same little girl having to clamber 5A's even steeper stairs for six days straight without injuring herself.

---

22 The age gap between Madeleine and her siblings was one year and eighteen-and-a-half months. As this narrative will demonstrate, the knowledge that Madeleine's birthday was just days away plays significantly into the narrative, just as Burke Ramsey's tenth birthday on 27th January, a month and two days after JonBenét's murder on Christmas night has significant import into the Ramsey case. [Note: Some reports indicate that the McCanns double buggy was present and accounted for, however the Ocean Club also had double buggies of their own.]

- On the afternoon of the 28th the McCanns head [no time given] to the pool area to join the rest of the holiday group [who will become infamous as the "Tapas Seven"] and who, according to Kate had arrived "a few hours" earlier. According to Kate, she and Madeleine swim together. The weather is "pleasant" although a cool breeze is blowing.

- Kate notes that the location of 5A facing the road made the apartment a "prime target" for opportunistic criminals. This echoes the Ramsey narrative, which had their neighbourhood in Boulder veritably crawling with burglars and paedophiles.

- Kate describes the rather Spartan interior as lovely, larger than expected and well-equipped. From crime scene photos it appears not only bare, but minimally decorated. Even so, Kate describes the hotel as "upmarket".

- Children booked into "kids clubs" for the next day.

- Dinner at Millennium restaurant half a mile from Ocean Club on the first night. It is not explicitly mentioned that the McCanns have dinner with the Tapas Seven that night, but from the fact that several tables are moved "so we could all sit together" we can infer that they did.

- Toddlers are weary from the long walk.

- Blinds and curtains are drawn and remain closed all week. Due to cold weather, windows remain closed all week.[23]

---

23 According to *Truth of the Lie* the window was opened: *"...on the glass, on the handle and on the right-hand frame of Madeleine's bedroom window, we had lifted five fingerprints - three from a middle finger and two from an index finger – all from a left hand, identified as belonging to Kate McCann. It had been cleaned the day before, May 2nd, by an Ocean Club employee, and the only fingerprints found were Kate's.... There is no doubt that somebody opened that*

- Madeleine enjoys "novelty" of sharing a room with her two bawling siblings.[24]

- Kate sums up the first day as feeling "mellow and content", and so it's an early mission accomplished for a great week together.

- Bed-time on the first night is indicated as "an hour behind schedule", so probably 20:30 or later.

April 29th [Part one]

- Family sleep well and wake up early [time unspecified], all feeling refreshed.

- Return on the half mile walk to the Millennium restaurant for breakfast.

- Meet Tapas Seven at Millennium restaurant [but don't walk there with them].

- Kate notes that she and Gerry wish to spend quality time together away from the children.

- Amelie, who seems to take after her mother Kate, is "unfazed" about being left at the Toddler's Club for two-year-olds. Sean, who seems to be more sensitive, and perhaps takes after Gerry, is initially "upset" at being abandoned.

- Madeleine is dropped off at Mini Club with her nanny, Cat.[25]

- Kate and Gerry head to tennis lessons. Both parents on their first morning in the Algarve, April 29th commit to a pre-arranged

---

window on the evening of May 3rd and the only fingerprints found on it were those of Kate [McCann]."

24 It's unlikely that three babies all under four-years-old sharing a strange room and strange beds in a strange place would have all slept soundly, especially on their first night in the Algarve.

25 Catriona Treasa Sisile Baker, childcare worker employed by the Ocean Club.

schedule of group tennis lessons for the rest of the weeklong holiday.

- Midday: Kate fetches the children.

- <u>Gerry heads to Baptista,</u> a medium-sized shopping centre, on his own to buy groceries. He buys cereal to negate the necessity of a long daily walk with the children to the Millennium restaurant and back for breakfast. This indicates that after just two visits to the restaurant, "walking" together wasn't an enjoyable experience for the McCann family.[26]

- McCann family have lunch with the Paynes and Diane Webster, enjoying the view from their upstairs balcony apartment.

- Afternoon: Kids dropped off at Kids Clubs. McCanns, Fiona, David and Dianne spend an hour by the pool [Note, April 29th is also a possible opportunity for the "last photo."]

- Kate and Gerry run together on the beach. The run to the beach and the return provide both parents with a mental "roadmap" on how to quickly get from the Ocean Club to the beach and back *on foot*. In addition, it allows both to establish how long covering various distances over the urban fringe between the sea and the hotel would take.

- The McCanns book adult-only dinner reservations at the more conveniently situated Tapas restaurant. It has a capacity for fifteen, perfect for the Tapas Nine.

- Kate cites the utility of this arrangement being that the kids could go to bed at their usual time with no fuss. [The only difference would be that the parents wouldn't be around *after* bed-time].

---

26 If walking with the family wasn't an enjoyable experience, jogging and running without them – possibly – was.

- Although the Ocean Club has a crèche facility [open 19:30-23:00] the McCanns [and possibly some or all of the Tapas Seven] in their wisdom as a group of doctors, decided not to use it.[27] Instead, the doctors went for the far less convenient "musical chairs" scenario which was to have their children in a remote [if relatively nearby] location and regularly interrupting their dinners to do their "child-checking" themselves. Yes, far more convenient than using a crèche…

A croaking maniacal laugh grinds the ear drums and turns blood cold from somewhere just above. After that rude noise, there is no other sound save the defeated sigh of the sea. There are no wings floating into the pitch black. There is no glint. Nothing.

Deep inside the black hole circling above is the silhouette in the shape of a small dark cross. It is held aloft, though not very high above the Earth, over the slick black sea by the Lady of the Light. Though her remade medieval lines are veiled in impenetrable night, the wrought iron perch rises into the sky, a tiny arrow into maelstrom. It seems to quiver faintly in the dark for just a moment following the raven's disappearance.

Then the enormous maw opens blacker than black around it. And then all is completely still.

---

27 The reason cited for not using the crèche facility was that it opened when their children needed to be asleep. This sounds like potentially the worst reasoning ever – surely a crèche for sleeping children should open at bed-time, and leave the bother and nerve-frazzling process of putting toddlers to bed to the poor nanny. The ease with which the McCanns and their colleagues dismissed this facility does cast suspicion on the peculiar situation of having so many doctors in a family group. Why wouldn't a group of doctors see sedation of their children as an easy alternative to using the hotel's crèche?

THE RAVEN'S SILENCE

"Silence is better than unmeaning words."
— Pythagoras

Musical Chairs

"Silence is a true friend who never betrays."
— Confucius

The fact that both of the McCanns were doctors, as well as the cabal they hung out with in the Algarve, plays significantly into this narrative. That's not headline news. What's under-reported, I believe, are the ages of both doctors at the time of Madeleine's death/ disappearance [39] and the commitment to physical fitness of both her parents.

Gerry and Kate are a striking couple, one might even say an attractive couple, but as we so often see in true crime, the vanity involved in keeping up appearances sometimes becomes a fault line for a festering narcissism. It's wonderful when everybody loves you, you can do no wrong. So, what happens if or when you do make a mistake? When everybody loves you and your life is finally coming together, how easy is it to stop the bus and admit to making a monumental mess of things?[28]

---

28 John and Patsy Ramsey were involved in back to back party celebrations, many of them celebrating John's business success just prior to the Christmas-murder of their daughter in 1996. O.J. Simpson enjoyed immense popularity throughout his life, including from the opposite sex, prior to the double murder in Brentwood. Oscar Pistorius, especially in the six months prior to murdering his girlfriend [following his triumphant 2012 Olympics in London]

The final year of one's 30's is, at least psychologically, an important one. Efforts are made to hold onto one's youthfulness, and also, to an extent, certain freedoms.

> *"Fuck off. I'm ~~not~~ here to enjoy myself."*

That both Gerry and Kate dedicated so much of their holiday to babysitters and tennis provides a glimmer, perhaps, into their mutual motivations.

The remainder of the countdown to the disappearing act involving Madeleine provides a more tangible sense of routine than the first two days. The routine we see emerging just prior to May 3rd is important to juxtapose against May 3rd. What happened on May 3rd that was just like every other day? What wasn't?

April 29th [Part two]

- At around 17:00[29] Madeleine's Mini Club arrive near the Tapas restaurant to have their tea while their parents hover nearby, either playing tennis or sitting at the bar.

- After tea the parents hang out with their kids in the nearby play area for half an hour. The sky above the play area is clearly scattered with grey cloud. Notice, long sleeve shirts worn by all except the bald dude in the background.[30]

---

was an international media darling.

29 Shadows on the grass in the playground image indicate it was well past midday.

30 There is also controversy around the playground photo. It appears someone is taking a photo through the shaded area of the playhouse. The bald man has been identified as a police officer, as an Ocean Club guest [Rajinder Balu or Neil Berry] while others speculate it might be Jamie Pyatt, a reporter from *The Sun*. What's also odd about the image is the bottom of the bald guy's trousers, which seem to show his

- After half an hour at the playground, the kids return to the apartment feeling tired, presumably accompanied by both parents, although this is far from clear.

- Kate establishes the twin's regular bedtime as shortly after seven, and Madeleine's as a half hour later.

- Kate establishes that by eight 'o clock all the children are usually sound asleep, and further that Madeleine has outgrown her chronic insomnia suffered by one and all when she was a toddler.

- Kate describes the bedtime ritual as a familiar routine on just their second night in the Algarve. Since the first night violated the schedule, the second night was effectively the first day to begin establishing the ritual, and thus it could only be established from the third night onwards.

- Kate and Gerry shower and settle down in private to share a bottle of wine together before joining the Tapas Seven at eight thirty. [Of course, if they were drinking wine they could have gone out to drink wine at the Tapas bar. If they weren't drinking wine it's possible they spent the hour trying to get the children, especially Madeleine, to settle].

- Kate clarifies that they could have hired a babysitter, but wouldn't doing so in a strange place with an unknown babysitter be just as risky? She adds that the time distance from the bar to the apartment is 30 - 45 seconds, and repeats the mantra used in many of their subsequent interviews, that leaving the children was no different to having dinner in their own garden at home.[31]

---

shoe pointing in the direction of the viewer.

31 The crucial difference is that they weren't at home and if the children cried they likely wouldn't hear them in a hotel setting, whereas in the more intimate and quieter confines of a home in the suburbs, they would.

- 20:30 ~~All Tapas Nine present and accounted for.~~ Matt has an upset stomach so he stays in with the kids. The remaining Tapas Eight settle in for a dinner together.

- Gerry and Kate return from dinner at 23:00. While the McCanns imply that the Tapas Nine all "nipped back" every half hour to check on their children, in fact neither Matt and Rachael nor Dave and Fiona did.[32] Kate emphasises the convenience of regularly interrupting their dinner as opportunities to go to the bathroom or to pick up warm clothing. What she fails to mention is the temptation, especially as the cold night went on and the wine took effect, to not *want* to check at an apportioned time. What she also fails to mention is when some parents have to check and others don't, the temptation to skip a turn also escalates.

"Fuck off. I'm ~~not~~ here to enjoy myself."

Kate concludes her narration of the last day in April by denying that they were partying wildly every night in Portugal. There doesn't need to be an extreme between staying in to look after children and wild partying for there to be a possibility of neglect. Even mild drinking each night [which was what the Tapas scenario entailed] meant a prolonged period where the children weren't directly supervised.

In a sense, the McCanns might as well have been partying wildly because if they weren't with their children, and no one else was, for

---

32 The Paynes had a high-tech baby monitor which allowed them to "listen in" on their children remotely. On April 29th Dr. Matthew Oldfield stayed behind in his apartment to look after Grace, his infant daughter of 19 months [the second youngest child of the entire group. Scarlett Payne, 11 months, was the youngest of all the children.]

blocks of time that repeated each night, then what would have been the difference?

April 30th [Apartment is cleaned]

- 07:00-07:30 McCanns and group awaken.[33] Breakfast at the apartment.
- Kids dropped off at Kids Clubs.
- Tennis lessons. [09:15 for Kate for one hour. 10:15 for Gerry for one hour].
- 11:00 – 12:00 Unknown.
- 12:00-12:30 Collect children and have lunch.
- Afternoon: Kids dropped off at Kids Clubs.
- Run/Tennis/Chatting ~~by the pool~~ in/near the Tapas restaurant.
- 17:00 Tea and then parents spend half hour in the playground area with children.
- Fun Tennis. [Ladies night on Monday]
- Kate heads to Baptista supermarket to stock up ahead of the public holiday on May 1st.
- Rachael books the entire group of nine into Tapas for 20:30 onwards for the rest of the week
- 20:30 All Tapas Nine present and accounted for. Cold wind blows.
- Bedtime not disclosed.

---

33 07:00-07:30 was given as the default time everyone woke up each day.

May 1st

- 07:00-07:30 McCanns and group awaken. Breakfast at the apartment.
- Kids dropped off at Kids Clubs.
- Tennis lessons.
- Kate returns to apartment after her lesson at 10:15 to supervise **two handymen fixing the** washing machine and **shutters**.
- Madeleine and her Mini Club plays on vacant court beside Gerry's during Gerry's lesson.
- Kate runs back to apartment to get her camera and clicks the "tennis balls photo."
- 12:00-12:30 Collect children and have lunch.
- Afternoon: Kids ~~dropped off at Kids Clubs~~ taken to beach however the weather is foul.
- Ice-creams. Kate, though feeling "torn", leaves her three children sitting on a bench to help Gerry collect ice-creams.
- Madeleine asks to return to Kids Club.
- On the way, the family enter a shop to buy sunglasses for Gerry [An allusion to the sunglasses worn in the "last photo"?] Kate remarks that her memory of these details is accurate, and also refers specifically to being "armed" with "photographs" as a ploy to extract every iota of memory they could as accurately as they could.
- Kids dropped off at Kids Clubs at approximately 15:30.
- 17:00 Tea and then parents spend half hour in the playground area with children.

- Fun Tennis. [Object theme – where coaches are given non-tennis racquets used to return tennis balls.]

- 20:30 ~~All Tapas Nine present and accounted for~~. Russell absent all evening as Evie is ill. Cold wind blows. Jane takes his meal to him.

- Bedtime not disclosed.

- Madeleine awakens during the night complaining that Amelie had woken her up. Gerry settles Amelie. Madeleine is allowed to sleep with her parents in their bed.

This is an alarm bell for the obvious fact that sleeping with the twins for Madeleine wasn't a small matter, and even less so with her parents not around not just on one evening, but several. Had Madeleine awoken and found her parents gone, initially she might have laid there for a while, perhaps looked around, but if the circumstances repeated she might have grown more and more anxious as the week wore on. As we're about to see, this is *precisely* how it unravelled for three-almost-four-year-old Madeleine.

~

May 2ⁿᵈ

"Our lives begin to end the day we become silent about things that matter." — Martin Luther King, Jr.

K ate introduces May 2ⁿᵈ as the last "completely happy day" as a family of five. But was it really?

- 07:00-07:30 McCanns and group awaken. Breakfast at the apartment.

- Kids dropped off at Kids Clubs.

- ~~Tennis lessons.~~ Postponed due to rain.

- Apartment is cleaned by a housekeeper, including windows.

- McCanns join the Payne's <u>at the Millennium restaurant</u> for coffee [sans children].

- Kate goes for a run with Matt [presumably in the rain]. Time undisclosed.

- Dog jumps out from under a bench and ~~bites~~ attacks Kate's right calf. Kate continues running regardless.

- 12:00-12:30 McCanns collect children and have lunch.

- Spend an hour with them in play area.

- Kids dropped off at Kids Clubs.

- Gerry has rescheduled tennis lesson. [Exact time not disclosed.]

- Kate has rescheduled tennis lesson. [Exact time not disclosed.]

- 17:00 Tea and then parents spend half hour in the playground area with children.

- Fun Tennis. [Object theme – where coaches are given non-tennis racquets used to return tennis balls.]

- 20:30 ~~All Tapas Nine present and accounted for.~~ Rachael not well, absent all evening in the apartment next to McCann's.

- Couples venture into a warmer "enclosed" bar area for "a liqueur." McCanns delay their checks to 45 minutes as a result, which was out of the norm.

- Bedtime ~~not disclosed~~. For Gerry disclosed as 23:50, the latest for the entire holiday with the exception of the night Madeleine vanished. Gerry returns home alone.

"Fuck off. I'm ~~not~~ here to enjoy myself."

- Kate returns even later, <u>declaring herself "miffed" and "embarrassed" at Gerry</u> for leaving her there.

"Fuck off. I'm ~~not~~ here to enjoy myself."

- Kate does not sleep in the same bed as Gerry on the last "completely happy day" but makes use of the extra bed in the children's room. Describes Gerry as "my snoring husband".

For the uncritical, it may seem as though the McCanns were in an irrevocable routine from the moment they touched down in the Algarve, to the moment Madeleine vanished – out of the blue.

Peeling away the gossamer threads from the narrative we can see that over the course of just four days [April 29th – May 2nd] *very little* was routine: not the weather, not where they ate meals, not where or when they slept and not what did as a family.

It's also easy to ignore the fact that the three children were forced to adapt to their separate play groups. While they may have had some family friends in common, of the three McCann children, Madeleine was on her own [without her family] and on her own in Kids Clubs pretty much each day every day. To make matters worse, after being put to bed, she was on her own all over again. So, if an issue arose where Madeleine wanted to be in the comfort and security of her parents, how would that be resolved *if they were always somewhere else*?

It's subtle, but if you read the schedule carefully, what we want to piece together isn't what's there but *what isn't there*. Well, what isn't there? And there are two critically important absences from the "routine narrative". Something was wrong with this too-good-to-be-true happy picture when it was laid down ten years ago.

What was it?

We can see that almost every night someone amongst the Tapas Nine disappears to look after children. April 29th is the *only night*[34] where everyone is present and accounted for. I realise the McCanns – and for that matter the Tapas Seven – maintain that on May 3rd everyone was accounted for. If the Tapas Seven are correct, then the McCanns both have alibis. The thing is, no matter how you slice it, no one can be present and accounted for in a musical chairs scenario where there's a veritable relay of child-checking going on.

I'm not certain whether the McCanns or the Tapas Seven are explicit about the same arrangement on other nights [several adults getting up

---

34 On May 3rd the Tapas Nine were all present and accounted for according to Kate McCann. In her account, she names them in the chronology of their arrival with the McCanns claiming they arrived first "just after 20:30." However, there is some doubt whether this version of events is accurate. Reasons for this are provided in the final chapter.

to check on their children first-hand], but even if we give them the benefit of the doubt, we know the Paynes had a child monitor and on certain evenings parents stayed in. As such, only April 30th and May 3rd emerge as genuine opportunities for child checking relays for the entire group. Yet, when all nine are present and accounted for, it's not mentioned *in any detail* on April 30th.

The full absurdity of the "musical chair" arrangement becomes explicit on the night of Madeleine's disappearance. There are adults hopping up at the same time as other adults, and other times, someone takes over the "relay" for someone else.

"Fuck off. I'm ~~not~~ here to enjoy myself."

In Gerry's case, there's also leaving the complex, crossing to the far side of the road and stopping for a chat while food is on the way.

"Fuck off. I'm not here to enjoy myself."

Some of the group didn't need to check on their children [baby monitor] and others did. All this is a clearly confusing pattern for what is represented as an iron-clad "collective" one-size fits all arrangement conjured in the name of convenience.

It doesn't sound very convenient to me, but that's not what's setting psychological alarms off.

What was it?

Kate McCann is explicit on which of the Tapas Nine weren't present and accounted for on each and every occasion. And on each and every occasion, the McCanns are at the Tapas restaurant because *there's never a problem with any of their own children.*

Statistically speaking, because the McCanns had three children – the most in the group – the chances of their having an issue ought to have been the greatest. According to Kate's narrative, not once – to their knowledge[35] – did any of the McCann children have an issue while they had been out at the Tapas restaurant.

They also don't mention, during any of their multiple checks on April 29th, 30th, May 1st, or May 2nd arriving at the apartment to any sort of disturbance or any of the children awake or in any kind of distress.

According to the McCanns, and this is a key flaw in their story, at some time during the week everyone else's kids have settling issues prompting absenteeism from the Tapas restaurant except theirs.

And this brings us to an allegation that has been levelled again and again at the McCanns. What would explain not only there being no settling issues, but there being no settling issues all week with the three McCann children, all sleeping soundly in the same room?

A sedative explains four things, at least in theory:

1. That it was **unnecessary to supervise the children during the early part of the evening**. The McCanns are adamant that the early part of the evening [when they were AWOL from the apartment] absolutely didn't warrant any concern because the kids never awakened early; they only ever awakened later in the evening, if ever. This certainty and this "mechanism" was bizarrely idiosyncratic to the McCanns compared to the Tapas Seven.

2. It reinforces this idea of **an inviolable night-time routine**. That once settled the kids remained settled. Kate's narrative refers

---

35 According to an upstairs neighbour of the McCanns, Mrs Pamela Fenn [73] in 5G heard a child from the apartment below [whom she identified as older than an infant] wailing and yelling for an hour and fifteen minutes on the night of May 2nd. Media statements differ from police statements in that Fenn described the crying as happening on May 1st.

to the word "routine" 15 times, "settled" 15 times and "sleep" 39 times. There's a mismatch between Madeleine's chronic insomnia early on in her infancy and her ability to apparently sleep soundly in the Algarve.

3. Of the Tapas Nine, the McCanns were the only double doctor duo with **no obvious childcare back-up** in the Algarve. The Payne's had a granny [Dianne Webster] and a baby monitor to fall back on. Since they were two doctors, and since either there was a secret back-up [a sedative] or none [unlikely], it seems possible and even likely that a sedative was used. Since Kate was a former anaesthetist, she would have felt herself acutely aware of the practise of putting people to sleep particularly in a situation where someone else's stubborn sleeplessness may have impinged on the comforts of others, including Kate herself. Besides this, I realise it's not a scientific observation, but one gets a sense from both Gerry and Kate that neither liked to do chores unnecessarily. Kate wasn't thrilled with the idea of going to the Algarve initially, and both parents claim they left the child buggy behind to "travel light". Kate doesn't like the cold, or cold water. The greatest indictment of this "convenience" approach is the child checking service, not only because it *wasn't convenient*, but because – given what happened to Madeleine [no matter who was to blame] it didn't actually work.

4. This is jumping the gun slightly, but on the chaotic night of Madeleine's "abduction", despite a window open and puffing out blasts of ice-cold air, and despite family, friends and police stampeding through the apartment, the McCann twins slept soundly.[36]

---

36 Nine-year-old Burke Ramsey, JonBenét's older brother, was also said to be asleep by his parents while family and friends stampeded through the 120-year-old house [with wooden floors] before dawn. Burke Ramsey later claimed he was awake,

Besides the sinister exceptionality of the McCann children sleeping soundly each night [and apparently on May 3rd as well], and besides the fact that it was never necessary – apparently – for the McCanns to cancel dinner plans to attend to their children, there's another glaring hole in their story. It's glaring but it's also subtle.

Kate's insistence that there was a routine to speak of is right, but only in <u>one critical area</u>. Each and every night the kids were left at 20:30 by both parents. For Madeleine, this unsettling pattern became *increasingly* unsettling, and <u>prompted her to say to her parents on the morning of May 3rd</u>, the day she vanished forever from the Algarve:

> *"Mummy, why didn't you come when we were crying last night?"*[37]

_____

but lay in bed pretending to be asleep. When asked if he was curious to see what was going on, he <u>claimed unconvincingly that he was "not the worried type"</u> [while fidgety and anxious on camera], and also the sort of person that liked to avoid conflict.

37 Kate subsequently adapted what she said to police from: *"Mummy, why didn't you come when we were crying last night?"* to *"Why didn't you come when Sean I and cried last night?"*

~

5A to 4G

*"The twins were so excited when they came on the holiday
because they were sleeping in the same room as Madeleine.
Every night they were thrilled about going to bed."*
— Kate McCann, <u>Daily Mirror</u>, August 18, 2007

On the morning of May 4th, 2007, Madeleine appears in Portugal, then Spain, Morocco, and the rest of Europe. Soon she's in Latin America, then in Zurich, then a street corner in Rio. The lead investigator would liken this to the circle of a shockwave enveloping the planet with the epicentre right here: Vila da Luz [the Ocean Club].

One of the strangest things about this case compared to others I've investigated – with Lisa Wilson – is the virtual umbilicus tying the McCanns to the actual crime scene. This was an early bugbear – that the McCanns not only remained in Praia da Luz for four months after Madeleine vanished but *where* they stayed during those four months.

Try to imagine the scenario. While the Portuguese police are inundated with global sightings, the McCanns are sort of quietly hanging around the crime scene [they <u>move to an upstairs corner unit of neighboring block</u>, i.e. to <u>4G from 5A</u>].

According to Ocean Club manager Emma Knight, on the night of the abduction the McCanns were settled into the new apartment. But

Kate McCann's version is a little muddier, suggesting two cots were prepared for the twins <u>in the Payne's apartment</u> [5H, diagonally left and above 5A].

It beggars belief that having supposedly just been a victim of an abduction, that the McCanns would simply go upstairs from their original location, especially when another apartment well away from the street was available. Given the theory doing the rounds at the moment, that Madeleine's abduction was a botched burglary, by moving in with the Payne's, theoretically everyone was being put at risk.

Now, in a scenario where the McCanns were complicit in their daughter's disappearance, and consider the possibility implied in that – that her body still had to be moved to a "final resting place" – one can imagine the McCanns wanting to keep tabs on their apartment. Who was there, what were they doing, what had they found?

Of course, the cops immediately faced a tsunami of leads [false leads] which were impossible to investigate either simultaneously, and extremely problematic to work through systematically. We'll get to the smoke and mirror stuff, the media narrative and also the inconsistencies around the Tapas Seven. For now – with the exception of Jane Tanner's testimony – I don't want to dilute this narrative by following up on those leads merely to illustrate they don't get us anywhere.

As part of my due diligence, however, I will look into these areas in order to understand how the McCanns constructed their protective barrier – after all, guilty or innocent, the McCanns, like the Ramseys, were never prosecuted – and ultimately, they won their campaign. Once we've completed an initial sweep we will drill into those details. Make sense?

The hanging around the crime scene thing was something I found troubling and confusing from the start. I thought it might be idiosyncratic to an abduction, but wasn't convinced. The bottom-line is a crime has impacted on one's family and so the basic response ought to be making sure everyone is safe.

One could argue what the McCanns argued – that they would not leave the Algarve until they'd located their missing child. It's difficult to overstate the stupidity of this assertion.

The portrait Kate sketches of May 4th is of the well-to-do doctors from Britain who'd been living in an upmarket establishment with their well-to-do companions, being dragged into a basic and shabby station run by the Portuguese police. The cops were described as casual, smoking and bantering. Kate tries not to judge the disorganised station or the people in it, but then she does – she's appalled and "nervous."

When the McCanns speak to the police Kate describes it as laborious, and constantly looks at the clock. She complains that notes taken by an officer are jotted down on a loose piece of paper rather than scribbled into a notebook. If Kate wanted to undermine the cops – their most vital asset to getting Madeleine back – she could hardly have done a better job.

When they leave the station sometime after 20:30, they return to the Ocean Club, and Kate is bewildered by what she describes as a zoo of television crews, clicking cameras and reporters. Curiously John Ramsey uses precisely the same word in his book *Death of Innocence*, when describing the bogus seven hour long kidnapping phase.

"The house starts to feel like a zoo…"

Of course, the Ramseys themselves had invited four friends and a priest over, and had done this so quickly, they arrived almost before the police did. In the same way, Kate suggests that they were victims of a commotion, including in their own apartment [4G] which was "heaving with people" when they arrived home on the night following the disappearance.

Kate's mum, dad, and auntie are there, so is the British ambassador, the director of Mark Warner [John Hill], the hotel manager [Emma Knight], a PR crisis management specialist [Alex Woolfall], a British Embassy press officer [Andy Bowes] and various other persons with government credentials.

One may be impressed by the speed at which this army of interlocutors had filled up the 4G war room. One might also argue, where were the twins while all of this was going on? Did they know their sister had been abducted?

A far smarter response to a genuine abduction would have been for Kate and the children to immediately fly back to the UK, or to do so as soon as the Portuguese authorities were done questioning them. We saw precisely this from the "British girls" associated with the Amanda Knox investigation. Without exception, all of Meredith's friends bugged out and returned to Britain – wanting to be somewhere safe and familiar, and wanting the protection afforded by their country of domicile. Amanda Knox, however, despite her housemate's murder in the room next to hers, thought she could continue in Perugia as normal, and in fact, returned to attending classes at the university as soon as classes resumed. Had she forgotten a killer was on the loose?

In the aftermath of a crime, what we often see is either complete alienation or an odd "no big deal" response. The Ramseys abandoned their expensive Tudor home within minutes after JonBenét's body was discovered dead in the basement. They never returned to their home. Some have argued that innocent parents turn their children's bedrooms into a shrine, often changing nothing but sort of holding onto the room as a sanctum of memory. The Ramseys didn't, and like the McCanns, moved in – initially – with another family. Had they forgotten a killer was on the loose?

Oscar Pistorius, like the Ramseys, did not want to *ever* return to his home after turning his own bathroom into a bloodbath. But then, like the Ramseys, he soon converted the home to cash and the cash into legal fees. Part of that went into Oscar and his own sister doing a reconstruction of his home – something that would have been far easier to do inside his *actual* home. As much as Oscar and the Ramseys may have wanted to or needed to return home, they couldn't – it was a crime scene, and would remain so for months.

On May 19th, barely two weeks after Madeleine's disappearance, Gerry and Kate emerge from their "physical shutdown." They get up at 07:00, leave the twins with family to look after, and go for a jog together. They run to a monument – probably Porto de Mós – situated at the top of a steep cliff overlooking Praia da Luz. The trail is 4-5km long and the doctors reach it in a credible 19 minutes.

"Fuck off. I'm ~~not~~ here to enjoy myself."

About two months later the couple are in;. erviewed by Sky News. They're seated on a blue sofa much like the one in their original apartment.

"Fuck off. I'm not here to enjoy myself."

Google Maps allows unfettered access to Praia da Luz and the Ocean Club. At a glance, it's obvious the Ocean Club is pretty standard fare. Google gives the hotel a three-star rating, and its reviewers give it an even lower rating [2.1 out of 5 stars]. As such, Ocean Club is hardly upmarket. If anything, it's average, providing the bare minimum in facilities and amenities.

This is important to bear in mind when we consider the media deluge that engulfed Portugal, and with it, this impression of decent, wealthy, well-to-do doctors being victimised by a cold and backward second class country.

It's easy to forget the McCanns chose Portugal[38] for their holiday, chose it in the off-season and chose an average hotel and cheap hotel room [with no view] for their family vacation.

It's also easy to forget that the McCanns in May – between trail runs and visits to the beach – invited not only the dignitaries inside 4G, but the media as well,[39] into their world.

---

38 On 1 January 2007 the idea of a group break to Portugal was first floated by David and Fiona Payne. Technically it was the Payne's idea but everyone in the group signed up for it.

39 Both the McCanns and the Ramseys accused the police of leaking confidential information to the media. However, in both cases the police were under the cosh thanks to strict secrecy laws in Portugal, and a strict media embargo in Boulder. Ironically the police accused their opponents, prime suspects in the incidents involving their daughters, of taking the media into their confidence rather than co-operating with the police or with the investigation.

~

Blind Spots in the Rear-view Mirror

"I think we are blind. Blind people who can see, but do not see." — Jose Saramago

Looking back ten years after the events has many advantages. For starters, one has the entire reservoir of the case file at one's disposal to drain and absorb. But using hindsight as a tool has a downside as well. One tends to see the case confined from a sort of back seat and "rear-view" perspective. It may seem as though one can see *everything* at a glance, but as you well know, appearances – especially when it comes to true crime – can be deceiving.

When using hindsight, the rear-view works as a sort of spatula that picks up a lot but unfortunately, many of the vital little nuances stick to the frying pan. Given that time moves forward, the more time that passes, the more hidden and eventually buried, these subtleties become. They're there, and they're in abundance. For the purposes of this narrative, I'll illustrate just one.

On April 10th, 2008, barely eleven months after the media shitstorm blew from the Algarve over Britain through Europe and the rest of the world, *The Sun* reported on Madeleine sobbing while left alone on the night before her abduction.

From shakedowntitle.com:

"...*Madeleine McCann asked why Kate and Gerry had not gone to comfort her as she cried the night before she vanished, according to reports. The four-year-old is said to have asked why mum Kate, 39, had left her and her twin siblings... to sob alone in their room the previous night. The Spanish TV station Telecinco made the claim as it broadcast translated copies of documents it said were the McCann's police statements. Crime reporter Nacho Abad, read out in Spanish an excerpt of the statement he said Kate had given Portuguese police...The reporter also told how Gerry revealed to police in his statement that workmen had come into their holiday flat to fix a broken window shutter in the main bedroom two days before she went missing.*"

In the Ramsey case the first suspects brought to the attention of the police by JonBenét's parents were the housekeeper [who sued the Ramseys to clear her name], Santa Claus and Mrs Claus [also employed by the Ramseys] and several employees working for John Ramsey's company Access Graphics.

Amanda Knox, a waitress at the time of Meredith Kercher's murder, falsely implicated her boss to police [and Patrick Lumumba , who lost his Le Chic club due to bad press, later sued her too].

It seems the natural flow of the criminal narrative is to start by implicating an employer or employee and if nothing sticks, to then lump everything on police bungling.

Now, as I've noted earlier, media reports and police statements differ on the date of Madeleine's crying episode. The police statements have Madeleine and her siblings sobbing alone for over an hour on May 1st, while the media [understandably] seem to have interpreted this as lost in translation, and gravitated to the McCann version – that it happened on May 2nd. Obviously if it happened earlier and the McCanns failed to respond for the next two days, that's more egregious neglect than if it happened the night before she disappeared.

But arguing over whether Madeleine cried on the 1st or 2nd misses the point – the little girl was aware she was home alone and very distressed before she disappeared. Her parents knew this and didn't appear to change their routine either way.

From shakedowntitle.com:

The Technical Services Director of the Ocean Club resort, Silvia Batista, affirmed that the same night on which Madeleine disappeared, she in person offered child-minding services "because the hotel is responsible for its clients' children, but they rejected that."

This is broadly indicative of the fact that, whatever the McCanns maintained, others seemed to know that their children were crying and unattended. Given the cheek by jowl juxtaposition of the Ocean Club's apartments, as well as the lower apartments protruding beneath the upper, one can safely assume sound didn't only travel but could be located with reasonable accuracy. It's hardly surprising then that Pamela Fenn – directly above the McCanns – heard and was bothered by over an hour of constant wailing.

Naturally, this narrative flies in the face of Kate's contention of completely happy days. What's also telling is how Kate frames Madeleine herself: in the middle of relating the painful incident of being left alone, Madeleine apparently moves on to another topic. It's no big deal. But it's a little tricksy of Kate to hijack her daughter's narrative, I think.

Burke Ramsey as a ten-year-old, and just thirteen days after his sister's murder, uses the same completely disassociated language to describe himself "getting on with life" when asked how he was coping after JonBenét's death. Oscar Pistorius similarly hijacks the narrative of the woman he murdered. During his sentencing phase he went on television to say Reeva wouldn't want him to waste his life behind bars.

What these gimmicks have in common is a concerted effort to manipulate the narrative, and to do so in a way that minimises the victim and maximises the suspect. But what's interesting, and what needs proper airing, is how this plays out in the media.

In the same article published in *The Sun* citing the sobbing incident for the very first time – on May 10th, 2008 – the McCann's spokesman is on the warpath, angry about the leak potentially jeopardising the investigation or infringing on the rights of his clients. One must see this in its proper context though, which is easy to miss through the rear-view mirror.

It has taken almost a year for the fact of Madeleine's crying to even enter the narrative. Naturally this is damaging to the McCanns, but think about the fact that the McCanns themselves – by hook or by crook – have avoided disclosing this detail to the media themselves. Notice also that it is disclosed by literally reading the McCanns own statements to police. So, there can hardly be an allegation of word twisting or manipulating the narrative. If anything, the idea is to reset the narrative, to align it with another version of the story. What does Clarence Mitchell think about that?

From shakedowntitle.com:

Today the McCann's spokesman Clarence Mitchell said the couple were very concerned about the leak. Speaking as he returned from a trip to Brussels with them to lobby the EU for a missing child alert system, he said: "I am not going to confirm or deny the content of any statements Gerry and Kate have made. But we are extremely concerned such material, if it is authentic, has apparently been leaked."

Now we know that the "leak" as Mitchell called it was authentic, it's in Kate's book, so by 2011 even the McCanns had added it to their own narrative [if not before].

From shakedowntitle.com:

The McCanns are thought to have spent several nights eating tapas at a restaurant near their holiday complex while their children slept alone in their apartment.

The station claimed Gerry, who checked on the children at 9pm, told police: "I saw the angle of their door had changed and it was open around 45 degrees. I thought perhaps Madeleine had woken up and left the room. Out of the corner of my eye I looked in our room and couldn't see her. Then I opened the children's door 60 degrees and looked to the left and saw Maddie sleeping with her head on the pillow on the right hand side of the bed. She was breathing softly and I thought how beautiful she looked. I thought it was quite hot and I didn't need to cover her up."

There's a shit ton wrong with Gerry's statement to police. I won't go into the merits in detail now except to observe:

1. In Gerry's version to police he "opens the door" to the idea of Madeleine getting up and walking somewhere of her own accord. It's subsequently revealed that Madeleine was in the habit of doing so. [Err…isn't May 3rd a little late to become concerned that Madeleine might be ambulating through the unlocked apartment on her own…?]

2. Why does Gerry need to look out of the corner of his eye? Why not just look?

3. Why is the door opened 45 or 60 degrees? [We'll get to this in due course, but this peculiar geometry lesson with doors seems to ~~allow for the possibility~~ leave the door open to the alternative that someone could have been inside the apartment hiding behind the door.]

4. The minimum temperature on May 3rd was 13 °C, that's hardly "hot." By mentioning this Gerry seeds the listener's mind with

the idea that the window couldn't have been open then if the apartment was "hot."

The Ramseys, Amanda Knox and Oscar Pistorius also populate their yarns with issues of hot and cold, open windows and closed balcony doors. The purpose of this is to open the door – or window – to allow phantoms to have the run of their homes.

In all four of these narratives, there's the suggestion of a burglary gone wrong. It's not murder, it's a burglary. It's not murder, it's a kidnapping. Nobody died, someone was abducted. This minimising manipulation of the narrative is echoed in a matching minimising of the victims themselves.

Just over six years after Madeleine's disappearance, and five years following the initial "leak", the Express publishes a new spin on the sobbing episode.

From shakedowntitle.com:

It is already known that Pamela Fenn, who lived directly above apartment 5a, heard a child, believed to be Madeleine, crying for about an hour on the evening of May 2. She was so concerned she rang a friend in the village to ask what to do and considered ringing Portugal's Policia Judiciaria. At the time, Madeleine's mother Kate and father Gerry were dining with friends at a tapas bar some 50 yards from the apartment.

A source said: "Police were astonished when this new information came to light. Officers spoke to other key witnesses to discover more about the middle-aged couple. Apparently they were concerned about the crying and went to see if they could comfort the girl."

Pamela Fenn has since died, so police have been speaking to other people who were staying in the same apartments.

Now, you may notice there are no objections to this story from Clarence Mitchell, and also, with Fenn's passing, a new narrative has been floated of a mystery couple arriving at the scene to comfort Madeleine. This is confusing because why would a mystery couple abduct Madeleine? Oh well, perhaps for her own protection? Or perhaps these phantoms saw something that night, or someone, that can expand the suspect pool exponentially. Perhaps not an egg with hair but a coconut with a beard?

Notice also where the "revelations" [not leaks] come from. When Scotland Yard shares its findings to the British press [which support the McCanns as innocent victims] then it's all above board. When the Portuguese do the same [and paint the McCanns as suspects, even using their own words], then there's a leak and there's hell to pay.

From shakedowntitle.com:

Our revelation comes as Scotland Yard detectives say there are potentially 20 suspects they want to speak to. Retiring Detective Chief Superintendent Hamish Campbell, head of the Yard's Homicide and Serious Crime Command, urged Portuguese authorities to investigate the new leads.

He said: "There are a lot of people of interest. There are people who could be properly explored further, if only to be eliminated."

The message is quite simple: there are 20 more leads to investigate, which means 20 potential people besides the McCanns.

Thank you very much, much obliged, but as much as the Portuguese respect their superior and better informed British counterparts, they're not going to chase their tails or conduct any additional wild goose chases. And so, Madeleine remains missing and the cold case enters its winter phase.

PR and the Premier League
[Mid-May 2007 onwards]

"Laughter lights up the darkness." — A.D. Posey

T he winter phase of any criminal case is that long, drawn out period where an investigation basically gets frozen. There's no progress, although often, it may appear as if many things are happening.

In winter, as living things revert to inertia, it may look like things are happening. Snow falling may transform entire landscapes, hoar frosts may turn gardens into silver wonderlands. But under that glistening <u>beatificence</u> there's nothing. There's just cold, rigid, dead Earth.

The point of PR for a defendant is to field an opposition to a police narrative, especially one painting the defendant as a suspect.

1. PR as a Power Tool

The original start to this narrative focused on the peculiar media monster that lurks around this case. Since the media narrative involved in this case is so *peculiarly* massive and so convoluted, it was tough to know where to begin. With celebrities or <u>soccer players</u>?

In the end I pulled out a single piece of the pizza – the McCann's impact on the sports media [football in particular] – and held that up as <u>exhibit A</u>. Look, <u>notice all the toppings</u>. Notice how perfectly <u>each slice has been crafted</u>, the dough <u>baked to perfection</u> with <u>nothing overlooked</u>.

From there I wanted to take the narrative through the meat and potatoes of the tabloids. How day by day for six straight months, stories were farmed out, until the McCann case became media gold.

As I invested more and more effort into this aspect of the narrative, I found myself increasingly swallowed up by it, and soon I was swilling further and further away from the case itself. The tides had swept me so far and the currents were so strong, that I couldn't get back to the actual case. And so, I torpedoed the entire beginning. I stripped it out, turfed it out and started again.

Ironically, the second start also involved the media except I'd learned to push them to the background in order to keep the McCanns on stage, front and centre.

The "last photo" narrative threatened to do the same – to steer the narrative into murky conspiracy theory and away from matters at hand. The McCann case isn't a difficult case to deal with once one surgically removes the media narrative, and with it, all the muddy abduction stuff. It has this in common with the Ramsey case, and the legions of phantom kidnapping suspects associated with that case.

But now that we're here, and now that we're dealing with the PR aspect in a single cordoned off chapter, it's perhaps an opportune time to ask why it's done, what it achieves and precisely how it works.

First of all, it's important to understand the crisis situation the McCanns faced when Madeleine died/disappeared. I've provided some insight into their finances, but basically, they faced a situation of potential ruin. Their reputations as doctors could have been permanently ruined. Their ability to maintain custody of their precious twins was hanging in the balance. So, at midnight on May 3rd, 2007 the McCanns [I think] had to make a call – to come clean and face enormous and unknown damage [lose all they had worked for so long to accumulate, including their brand-new house in Rothley] or to hold onto everything they could [like the new house] and fight the charges, the suspicion, the questions and the investigation with all they could muster.

If this seems a stretch, consider the Ramseys, Oscar Pistorius, O.J. Simpson, Amanda Knox, Damien Echols [of the West Memphis Three] and Steven Avery's use of PR as a tool to control the narrative. Of these prime suspects and convicted murderers mentioned, at least half beat the charges against them and virtually all of them ultimately escaped maximum sentences. The Ramseys, O.J. Simpson[40] and the McCanns escaped or avoided successful prosecutions, and the Mccanns and the Ramseys escaped prosecution entirely, which is an impressive trick [or earnest campaign] to pull.

Why is publicity used? It's an effective tool to exert pressure on an investigation. It's also an amazing tool to exert power, and to propagate power.

The legal system has a flaw in that the police and prosecution side are held to very high standards in terms of the verity of statements communicated to the media. These must necessarily be provable and if not, can be used against them in a court of law. Suspects, on the other hand, are typically the most newsworthy beacons in high profile cases, which means the media fall over themselves to get a first-hand comment or quote. There's no requirement to test or filter or even investigate the information, which means the untested unfiltered defendant's narrative typically dominates any sort of case.

---

40 OJ was acquitted on double homicide but was later convicted for aggravated burglary and sentenced to 33 years. The latter charge was seen by many as "payback" for an acquittal that many felt was undue.

This only changes once the case goes to trial. The verdict then essentially carves the narrative into stone. In a real sense the court case [whatever may happen within the trial narrative] is the ultimate controller of narratives.

What does the roping in of media and legions of supporters achieve beyond the attempt to control the narrative? In the Ramsey case, we see an incredible example of a *human barrier* created at a crime scene. The police are called to investigate a 911 call, but have to tippy toe respectfully for hours around a small flock of affluent folk grieving and engaged in prayer.

In the end, the failure to throw the people out who didn't need to be there, or move the people to the police station for questioning as soon as the Ramsey house became a crime scene, critically undermined their case. In other words, the barrier worked.

Virtually the moment the Ramseys [the prime suspects at that time, and for several years later] exited their home and out of police custody, they were able to excuse themselves from interrogation by citing medication, grief, having drank too much whiskey [in John Ramsey's case] and finally their legal right to a fair interrogation.

During the four months, the police battled to get the Ramseys to the station to submit to questions, the police also had to deal with a massive PR campaign painting them as inept bunglers who weren't doing enough to go after the real criminals. Every tick of the clock played into the Ramseys' favour.

The media also provides a barrier, but more in the form of pressure. If the police exert pressure on suspects, it helps the suspects if there is pressure exerted on the police as well. The more pressure exerted on the cops, the less resources the cops have to exert constant pressure on their suspects.

Prosecutions are an expensive process. Policing costs money. In the end, it's often a money game, a resource war. Whoever develops the more resilient war chest can buy the resources and soldiers needed to hold the fort. When a side runs out of resources, the battle turns. Many battles are waged on sentiment, and if the tabloids are on your side, so is the popular sentiment and the treasure.

So, we can see there are very real benefits to bringing the media onto the playing field if one is a defendant. Taking the football analogy further, an offense is a good defense, and if attack is sometimes the best form of defense, then you want the best and biggest offense possible. Well, in May Britain was enveloped in football fever. So why not infiltrate that narrative? Have countless heaving stadiums supporting poor Missing Madeleine. Best of all, even Portuguese players [under contract in England] could convert potentially hostile crowds back home…

2. Playing in the Premier League

Just five days after Madeleine's disappearance in the resort town of Praia da Luz, Cristiano Ronaldo, a Portuguese footballer playing for Manchester United at the time and one of the most famous footballers in the world, made a televised appeal on MUTV:

"*I was very upset to hear about the abduction of Madeleine McCann and I appeal for anybody with any information to come forward. Please come forward.*"

On May 11th, eight days after Madeleine vanished from her bed in her apartment at around 22:00 in the Algarve, David Beckham stepped up to make his public appeal. Holding up a poster with a photo of Madeleine, Beckham intoned:

"*If you have seen this little girl… please could you go to your local authorities or police and give any information that you have. Please. Please help us.*"

When <u>a picture of Madeleine was released wearing an Everton shirt</u>, two of Everton's Portuguese footballers made their appeals to the public. Next the team captain, Phil Neville made a statement on behalf of the club:

"Everton has fans all over the world and I know that they, along with everyone connected with the football club, are hoping and praying for Madeleine's safe return. Our thoughts are very much with the family at this extremely distressing time."

Everton's club manager David Moyes assured their supporters that his *"thoughts and prayers are with the family. If anybody out there knows anything, please come forward."*

And so, it went on. On May 12th, to mark Madeleine's fourth birthday, Celtic went onto the field against Aberdeen wearing yellow armbands.

On May 16th Spanish football fans in Glasgow for the 2007 UEFA Cup Final became a captive audience for a video appealing for help. Three days later, <u>at half-time during the FA Cup Final another film clip was shown</u> appealing for help. On May 21st, a Monday, the Liverpool team – on the eve of their departure for the 2007 UEFA Champion's League Final – held up a banner to press photographers appealing for information on Madeleine's disappearance.

At Lords, England's cricket team wore yellow ribbons while battling the West Indies. Madeleine's picture was also beamed onto the big screen above the oval.

In May 2007, it was clear Madeleine [but more specifically the McCanns, who were still in the Algarve, mostly[41]], ruled the airwaves. But something far more powerful and sinister was rising through the ether.

---

41 Gerry McCann returned to Britain without Kate on May 20th but returned to Praia da Luz two days later. Clarence Mitchell, still a government employee then, arrived in Praia da Luz with Gerry on the same day.

The first sign of this came from the Find Madeleine website, which pulled in 58 million hits in its first two days online. An unstoppable force was rising from the seabed like Moby Dick out of the Cape St. Vincent trench.

While one narrative caught on in British newspapers, making the front pages of several tabloids every day for almost six months, another narrative brewed and swilled in an altogether untested medium in 2007. The white whale rose through the virtual depths and while something flapped in the pale blue virtual sky. The McCanns didn't see it coming but then, who on Earth could?

THE RAVEN RETURNS

"I've begun to realize that you can listen to silence and learn from it. It has a quality and a dimension all its own." — Chaim Potok, The Chosen

Enter Goncalo and the Inexorable Rise of the Fail Whale

*"To...the thousands of anonymous citizens of
different nationalities, who have from the beginning,
and in many ways, expressed their solidarity [and]...
to [the] bloggers and surfers and others who defended
the cause of truth and justice."* — Goncalo Amaral

The Raven is hatched in Viseu [pronounced Vi-Sew], far to the north of the Algarve, in an ancient place where ancient roads and ancient people intersected. The old city which always remained a compact city [its population remains less than 100 000 today] gave rise to kings, nobles and conquerors.

The Renaissance painter Grão Vasco – whose sublime works included Jesus in the house of Marta, and the man who contributed to the iconic St Peter on his throne [1530] – hailed from the same place.

The city is famous for its wine, and otherwise notable today for its bright glassy edifice rising out of crumbling courtyards like a sword where the very dust is radioactive with human history.

Almost a thousand years ago, the man who would be its first king founded Portugal itself. Alfonso also hailed from these fertile winelands; before him ceaseless cycles of roving Celts, <u>Lusitanians</u>, Moors, Muslims and Visigoths. The Romans settled the area during eras of prosperity. When these eras unravelled, Christians came and Moors, and the new rivals knuckled down to siege tirelessly against one another with the sun-baked countryside around Viseu on the cards as a floating trophy.

From the faraway time of proto-history, to the Trump era we know as "post truth", the land and its inhabitants spun through successive occupations. Until one day, 48 years before the McCanns visited the Algarve, the Raven hatched in the village of <u>Torredeita</u> just outside Viseu. The Raven spread its wings over the country and grew to know its seasons, its fields, its subtleties.

Between 1992 and 1997 Amaral studied at Lisbon's Faculty of Law, taking night classes. A year later he took an investigation course affiliated with the Polícia Judiciária and graduated first of 100 students.

In his pursuit of the criminal underworld, the Raven haunted Lisbon, the Algarve and the Azores. He pursued it all – robbery, murder, drug trafficking. Violent crime. Organised crime. And in time, as some sort of weariness set in to his feathers, he made his way to the almond trees of the Algarve, settling in <u>the southern city of Portimão</u>.

This seaside enclave was half the bustle of Viseu [population 55 000] but with a vibrant shipbuilding, fishing and tourist industry. <u>Portimão is powerboating. The Portuguese Grand Prix of the Sea, a powerboating contest,</u> is held every year in Portimão. It was a place, the old bird might have imagined, to slow down, build a nest egg for his family of five [including three daughters] and eventually, retire.

Little did the black bird from Portimão know that in the spring of 2007, when Amaral was in his 26th year as a career detective, another family of five had touched down at Faro and were winding their way past Portimão towards Praia da Luz. Fate, it seems, is not without a sense of irony.

The families on that bus, just the same, had no idea that down the road behind the sign and the turn off to Portimão lived a tough Portuguese detective who couldn't speak or understand English. He would be the foil for the doctors, and the doctors would in turn be his.

Fortunes would be made and lost, and these doctors and detective stood at the very heart of it. And yet neither side would have any idea what sort of impact little blue birds would have on the invisible landscape beyond the almond trees, on the other side of spring and even summer.

In May 2007 the launch of Twitter in March of the same year would have felt like a galaxy far, far away to the doctors and the detective. And yet the incredible pulling power of the McCanns website, drawing tens of millions in just two days, ought to have been sufficient warning.

Somehow the clockwork of their massive media effort was unwinding. Some began to wonder, is this story [terrible as it was] just *too good to be true*? And increasingly those doubts, unacknowledged in the media, began to filter through a completely new medium. As summer wore on and the actual case turned to winter, the blue birds of social media began to chirp. First one, and then another...

~

Strange Dreams [July 2007]

"I decided it is better to scream. Silence is the real crime against humanity." — Nadezhda Mandelstam, Hope Against Hope

I n Kate's book, she writes about dreaming of Madeleine for the first time on September 1st, 2007. In the narrative, Kate admits to being confounded by the mysteriousness of the mind – why hadn't she dreamt of Madeleine before?

In the dream a nursery calls and informs Kate that Madeleine is there, and has been all this time. What's interesting about Kate's dream is even though she reconstructs Madeleine in fairy tale form, Madeleine's *still not there*. The whole dream is about Kate, and about what Kate feels. There's not a jot about Madeleine's disappearance, or expression or Madeleine saying anything [or Kate saying anything to Madeleine].

Kate seems to note nothing more profound than Madeleine – in her dream – looked as beautiful as she remembered her. Again, it's an odd psychological recycling that feels faintly off. Because how could this be a dream if it was little more than a re-envisioning; if it was a mere remembering disguised in a fake, frilly psychological dress?

What makes the dream in September even more inexplicable is the dream <u>documented in the media in July 2007 as Kate's "turning point" dream. Are you sure you want to hear this?</u>

From shakedowntitle.com:

Police Inspector Ricardo Paiva, who acted as a liaison between the McCanns and Portuguese detectives in the days following their daughter's disappearance, said [Kate's] dream was a "turning point" in the investigation.

<u>What are you talking about man?</u> Why would the Polícia Judiciária pay *any* heed to a mere dream?

From shakedowntitle.com:

*[Paiva] said that [Kate] told him in a tearful telephone conversation in late July 2007 that she had dreamt that **Madeleine was on a hill** and that police should search for her there. The claims came as Kate and Gerry McCann appeared in court to hear evidence on the first day of a hearing <u>to challenge the publication of a book</u> written by Algarve detective <u>Goncalo Amaral</u>.*

Ironic, isn't it? In their efforts to suppress information, the trial itself instead revealed previously unknown <u>inculpatory</u> evidence.

From shakedowntitle.com:

Insp Paiva told the hearing in Lisbon: "Kate called me, she was alone as Gerry was away and she was crying. She said she had dreamt that Madeleine was on a hill and that we should search for her there. She gave the impression that she thought she was dead – it was a turning point for us."

The dream itself wasn't relevant. What Kate had revealed was the psychology behind the dream. Kate had revealed a turning point in her own psychology. By communicating a new narrative to the police, not of an abduction, but death, the cops felt they'd been given the go-ahead to revert back to their original misgivings.

From shakedowntitle.com:

The senior detective said [Rocha Negra Cliff] was searched but nothing was found. "That is when we decided to send the specialist dogs in. British police informed us about how they could detect the scent of death."

He admitted that the police had been suspicious of the McCanns from the start of the investigation. Insp Paiva added: "They disobeyed our request to keep quiet about the details of their daughter's disappearance while we conducted our investigation. Instead they turned it into a media circus and that gave rise to some suspicions."

Paiva appears to be saying that by conjuring up a distracting circus, the cops grew more suspicious and distrusting of the McCanns than they already were. If they had been in any doubt, these doubts began to fester when Kate's dream and Krugel's opportune confirmation were conveyed in quick succession.

From shakedowntitle.com:

The officer in charge of the Polícia Judiciária inquiry, Inspector Gonçalo Amaral, interpreted Kate's support of Krugel as a ploy. By this point [Amaral] believed the McCanns were involved in the disappearance, and that Kate was using Krugel—she had also considered using psychics— to "disclose the location of her daughter's body" without compromising herself.

The cops requested specially trained sniffer dogs from Britain. While it's fairly well-known that the Spaniels "bingoed" in apartment 5A and around the McCann's rental vehicle, what's less well known is some media ignoramuses actually credited Krugel with finding traces of Madeleine on a beach.

From shakedowntitle.com:

Traces of Madeleine McCann's body were found on a Portuguese beach weeks after she was reported missing, during tests by a former detective renowned for locating abducted children.

Forensic analysis by retired South African police superintendent Danie Krugel claimed to reveal Madeleine's body had either been temporarily buried or was still beneath the beach at Praia da Luz, the resort from where she disappeared on 3 May. Based on a combination of Madeleine's DNA sample and GPS satellite technology, Krugel's findings were taken so seriously by Portuguese detectives that officers twice searched the beach.

For me the psychology that stands out isn't the nonsense surrounding Krugel, or the nonsensical dreams. The pertinent point is in Kate McCann's narrative. She makes zero reference to *any* dream about Madeleine in July. She'd dreamed her daughter was dead on a black mountain. It was significant enough for the retelling of that dream to become a turning point in the police investigation as early as July 2007. It was noteworthy enough to be raised in court. So why not write about it?

It's obvious though, isn't it? If the cops came down like a ton of bricks on the McCanns for that slip up, why compound the error in your own narrative? Well, you wouldn't if you were guilty. If you were innocent, of course you'd admit to moments where you had abandoned all hope. But to realise Madeleine was dead, and then, when the paw paw hit the fan in Portugal as a result, suddenly and conveniently – it has to be said – conjuring her back into the narrative certainly raises serious questions.

If anything, Kate alludes to this change in sentiment over the same period by having a chapter titled "The Tide Turns" along with obscure references to jogging juxtaposed with a "downward spiral."

I can't reiterate enough though, that what Kate left out of her narrative is an enormous big, stinking black hole especially when it had profound consequences for the investigation into their daughter as well as on Gerry. <u>Kate changed things!</u>

There's strong reason to believe while Gerry was away Kate's emotions ran away with her and she did something off-the-cuff, without telling Gerry about it. It's also important to note that the way Kate tells it she's incorrect at best and slyly dishonest at worst. By framing the September 1st dream as her first dream she neatly excises the July vision. This provides a prescient insight perhaps into just how meticulously the McCanns were in crafting and recrafting and recrafting their story.

To do our <u>due diligence as a devil's advocate</u> in terms of understanding the McCann's *actual* attempts to recraft their story, we need to examine a concrete example of their earnest attempt to pursue ~~their own~~ Madeleine's cause.

How did the McCanns investigate their own case? Is there even *one example* of a <u>balls to bones</u> investigative effort from their side?

As it happens, there is one. It involves one <u>Danie Krugel, a quack</u> from <u>Bloemfontein</u>, South Africa. The enterprising fellow armed with a tricorder, a moustache that could be mistaken for a thatched roof and an apparently cockamamie contraption was invited to the Algarve to work his magic. <u>This is him</u>.[42]

---

42 Actually, *this* is <u>Danie Krugel</u>.

~

Spock and his Tricorder to the Rescue!

"I never invite idiots to my house."
— Elizabeth Montagu

"The show is about to begin." — Goncalo Amaral's
reference to Danie Krugel's arrival in Portugal, in
mid-July 2007

Weeks pass after Madeleine's disappearance, and during that period, for Amaral's family at least – the Raven himself seems to disappear. Finally, his wife Sofia finds him brooding at his office in the Department of Criminal Investigation in Portimao. Sofia, his second wife, hugs him and hands him a flower basket. It brings a much-needed fragrance to Goncalo's drab office with its overflowing files, cigarette stubs and brimming ashtrays.

Between the orchids, lilies and roses are butterflies and birds decorated in green and yellow, the colors symbolising the search for Madeleine. Attached to the bouquet is a note from the Raven's daughters. Rita and Inès tell their father they love him and miss him and not to give up searching for Madeleine. But they also tell him, "Don't forget about us."

He lights a cigarette. In time the bouquet will wither and with it, any chances of finding Madeleine alive. It is precisely at this juncture, when

Sofia's hope-filled flowers had wilted and started decaying that a new player entered the game.

Kate McCann is the first to admit that roping Krugel into the investigation was mad. She provides evidence of this by quoting from her own diary entries. These entries basically confirmed the strategy was "ridiculous" but also noted that at that stage the McCanns had "nothing to lose." Well, actually, they did. They had Madeleine to lose unless she was already dead. If she was dead, of course, then yes, perhaps they had little else to lose.

Given the media campaign that was conjured out of the ether, seemingly at an instant, the McCanns didn't seem to be resting on their laurels. They seemed to be playing to win, and playing industriously which you either do when you've got nothing to lose or *everything* on the line.

If the McCanns had their backs against the wall [and I believe they did], if they weren't careful, they had their *own lives and livelihoods* to lose. In fact if they <u>didn't play their cards right</u> and <u>the case or the media really turned on them</u>, they risked losing their two remaining children too, and – it wasn't inconceivable – becoming the most hated couple in Britain. The stakes were about as high as they could get.

According to Kate, despite Krugel's specious claims, they were comforted by the notion that even a potentially crap investigation by a <u>kook</u> from the ass end of Africa was better than none at all.

Now, this may make a lot of sense to someone incapable of independent thought. For the rest, consider the scope of the irony here.

Consider the very real scenario that was playing out, and continued to play out for the entire lifespan of the case:

In the face of the irredeemable and boundless bungling of Polícia Judiciária, an ineptitude so chronic it had apparently reduced the McCanns to gnashing of teeth for Gerry and tears of frustration for Kate, and in the face of this, they were willing to invest their faith in a quackeroo.

Really?

Kate describes this period [a month and a half after Madeleine's disappearance] in her book as busy, mostly dedicated to coming up with [media] campaign ideas and replying to thousands of emails and letters. High priority stuff like that. It was into this eddy of activity that Krugel intruded.

On July 18th Kate was in the cop shop in Praia da Luz trying to get a handle on things. While a dodgy dude called Murat was occupying the McCanns [their pick then for "prime suspect" material] the Polícia Judiciária didn't have any hard evidence against him. Things were getting slippery. This lack of something concrete for her [or the media] to hold onto seemed to fill Kate with anger and rage [unless it was *actually* fear and loathing].

She describes herself feeling "possessed by some demonic alien." If so, she may not have been alone.

On June 9th, 2007, just a month and a week after Madeleine's disappearance, Danie Krugel enters the mythos of this story. It starts when Kate asks friends to visit her home in Rothley so they can collect some of Madeleine's hair. They are then to courier it to Bloemfontein, South Africa and Danie Krugel.

Krugel duly receives the hair, sets up his tricorder and immediately gets a reading. Madeleine [her remains at least] are in Praia da Luz! Krugel conveys this information to the McCanns, and on June 28th the McCanns summon the Krugel circus act to the Algarve.

They also seek to involve the Polícia Judiciária in Krugel's <u>larkum</u>. In *Truth of the Lie* Amaral is explicit about this:

"[The McCanns] want to make [Krugel's] intervention official and seek the agreement of the [Polícia Judiciária]."

To their credit, the cops don't fall for it. To the McCann's credit, this was potentially a brilliant ploy to discredit the Portuguese cops if that's what the exercise in futility was intended to do.

PORTUGUESE POLICE HIRE FRAUD TO FIND MADELEINE

Or:

PORTO PIGS PICK PSEUDO SCIENCE FOR MADDIE SEARCH

And if not to discredit the cops then to keep the media ball rolling. As long as it was rolling, the police and the public would be focused on the narrative in newspapers, not on them directly.

So, during the first two weeks of July arrangements are made to get the South African and his tricorder to Praia da Luz. Visas, flights and custom clearance need to be negotiated. [Krugel's fee as well, one assumes, but no one makes a peep about that.][43]

After making a scene in South Africa, customs allow the man and his machine through and Krugel, accompanied by a female journalist, heads to the epicentre of the Madeleine McCann case.

The 12 000 km flight from the bottom of Africa to the Algarve situated above the top edge of the continent takes Krugel between 13

---

43 According to an article in the *Mirror*, Krugel had a contract with an unnamed television company who filmed him while working on the Madeleine case.

and 15 hours,[44] with a stop in either London or Paris or possibly Accra, in Ghana if he's flying Transportes Aéreos Portugueses [Air Portugal or TAP]. During those dozen hours or more Krugel, the McCanns, the media and Amaral himself would have had ample opportunity to reflect on what was happening and why.

The cops and media would have had a chance to look into Krugel's record, and see that there was one [sort of].

Krugel first gained some semblance of recognition on <u>Carte Blanche</u>, a long running and <u>award-winning investigative television show</u> in South Africa. Dark haired, razor sharp Kimberly born <u>Ruda Landman, the daughter of two schoolteachers and one of the most recognised media workers in South Africa, filed this story</u>.

From <u>shakedowntitle.com</u>:

Episode title: Secret Science Tested

LANDMAN: *Can you remember when the fax machines first became part of the office set-up? When the computer replaced the typewriter? The first time you used an auto teller, the first cell phone call you made? It wasn't all that long ago, yet at the time it was mind boggling. Today it is the most common thing to do. You probably don't even think twice about it. Now imagine this: A person disappears, you find a few strands of hair left on a brush, you put those hairs into a gadget and that points out on a map where in the world that person may be. That's exactly what a group of Bloemfontein businessmen claim they are able to do. Steering the project is Danie Krugel, former police superintendent and current Director of Health and Safety at the Central University of Technology of the Free State.*

While Landman's new magic machine pitch fired up the imaginations of some South Africans, others were not so fired up.

---

44 There are no direct flights between Johannesburg and Lisbon.

From shakedowntitle.com:

It may have made for gripping viewing, but was it good investigative journalism, as it was purported to be? Carte Blanche's Sunday night documentary on the possible discovery of bones linked to the missing Van Rooyen girls has created a controversy, and probably not in the way it was intended.

The documentary has been both slammed by media critics and hailed by viewers as offering hope. Professor Anton Harber of Wits University's journalism school described the piece as "a bad joke told at the expense of the families involved". The hour-long piece, produced by award-winning journalist Susan Puren, was the result of two years of investigation, but does not come to a definitive conclusion.

So, in a sense, what Krugel offered the McCanns was something similar. A long period of investigation, a gripping narrative and then… an indefinite conclusion.

From shakedowntitle.com:

Months of meticulous research and investigation have culminated in a story so dramatic that details will only be divulged during the broadcast," the programme claimed ahead of the show.

The piece, presented by acclaimed journalist Ruda Landman, detailed how the unexplained disappearance of Tracey-Lee Scott-Crossley, Fiona Harvey, Joan Horn, Anne-Marie Wapenaar, Odette Boucher and Yolanda Wessels had remained in the minds of the public for 19 years. The disappearances were all linked to Pretoria paedophile Gert van Rooyen, who shot dead his girlfriend Joey Haarhoff and killed himself when they were cornered by police. The Carte Blanche team then linked up with former Free State policeman Danie Krugel, who claimed to have developed technology in which he is able to find the "master body" of something, using a sample consisting of the same DNA.

But how did this magic machine work?

From shakedowntitle.com:

Once the [DNA] sample is tested, Krugel's machine is said to pinpoint the main body containing the sought genetic signature using global positioning system (GPS) technology. Krugel claimed his machine readings, after tests done on hairs from two of the missing girls, pointed to a vacant plot of land situated six blocks from the Van Rooyen house.

Krugel's equipment was unable to pinpoint an exact location, narrowing down to a search area the size of two football pitches. Carte Blanche then contacted the owners of the land and were granted permission to conduct a forensic excavation on the property over the period of a week.

Now think about what we're talking about. There's a magic machine that can tell you where the remains of a person are. It tells you but also, it's a *little fuzzy* when it comes to accuracy. Two football fields in a suburban area is a nice chunk of fabric, the sort of range where so many children were likely to be disposed of in short order.

From shakedowntitle.com:

As days passed and no skeletons were found, Carte Blanche called on clairvoyant Marietta Theunissen...

[But] Harber said: "I am not sure what Carte Blanche was doing in this story, but it is not journalism. They base their report on two dubious characters – a clairvoyant and an ex-policeman with a mysterious super-machine – who led them to a patch of ground where they found a few unidentified bone fragments. This stuff belongs in a superhero comic, not in journalism."

Ultimately bone fragments were found in a nearby drain, but instead of them belonging to six missing schoolgirls the DNA belonged to four different adult males and two others. None of the samples could be matched but the state of degradation of two samples were such that they couldn't be conclusively ruled out either. And so, for some at least, Krugel got the benefit of the doubt. Dang it, the machine worked!

From shakedowntitle.com:

Dr George Claassen - a former head of the Stellenbosch University school of journalism and director of Sceptic South Africa - has been equally scathing in his analysis of the story.

He has publicly challenged both Krugel and Theunissen to allow their claims to be scientifically tested under controlled scientific circumstances in front of the Carte Blanche team.

"The abracadabra Theunissen speaks at the scene is so funny one would have thought Landman and Mazarakis had ventured into a new field of comedy writing. That any serious journalist could make her viewers believe that Theunissen has any credibility, is astonishing," Claassen claims.

But the seed had been sown and in 2007 it fell into the fertile soil of the McCann case.

From shakedowntitle.com:

A glance at the Carte Blanche website, where viewers' comments on the show are posted, shows that many people are now calling for Krugel to use his machine to find four-year-old Madeleine McCann, who went missing in Spain in May.

Now never mind that the South African reporter arguing for better investigative techniques got the country wrong where Madeleine McCann disappeared, what matters is Krugel had made it onto the media map, and either the McCanns picked him up on their radar, or they came up on his.

Landman, however, wasn't the female journalist accompanying Krugel to the Algarve. Many details surrounding Krugel's activities both in the Algarve and in South Africa seem to have been placed online and then erased after the fact. There are plenty of cached articles that come up on Google but have subsequently been pulled from various news sites.

What we do know is in 2007, <u>after presenting the show</u> for nineteen years, <u>Landman suddenly stopped working for Carte Blanche altogether.</u> Her final appearance on the show was on June 24ᵗʰ, 2007.[45] What we also know is instead of Landman accompanying Krugel it was Susan Puren, Landman's producer at Carte Blanche. So, another "award-winning South African journalist" had taken up the Krugel cudgel.

But before we get to Krugel entering customs in Portugal, and meeting up with Amaral himself, let's gather a little more from the man himself, in his own words to Landman.

From shakedowntitle.com:

KRUGEL: *If you get a signature sample of something… let's call it organic or non-organic… a very small sample. I have developed a method to use that small sample and to create data that I use to search for its origin. So, you transmit and you receive.*

LANDMAN: *Is there anything metaphysical involved? Are you psychic?*

KRUGEL: *I'm a Christian and I put it clearly… this is science, science, science! That is what is so fantastic about it. It is tied to the science we hear but people didn't realise it… it's just science. That's it.*

LANDMAN: *Given the massive potential of the invention, Danie refuses to divulge exactly how it works. He says the energy source is his most precious secret. Once he has done a test with a hair sample*

---

45 <u>Landman announced her decision</u> to quit in March 2007, indicating that her final appearance would be in June 2007.

– or signature material [which] pertains to whatever he's looking for – Danie is able to geographically pinpoint an area by applying co-ordinates from more than one vantage point. The search area is where the lines intersect.

In the past two years Danie's travelled across South Africa to test the equipment. This is a long list of his successes… [data on screen…]

LANDMAN: *How did you get involved in this area looking for people?*

KRUGEL: *I was following the Leigh Mathews case and that night on the news they said they had found her body. I was so upset. What bothered me was what went through her mind…The whole of South Africa was looking for her and nobody could help. That night I couldn't sleep.…*

So Krugel, keenly aware of a situation where an entire nation was turned upside down by a missing person scenario, wondered if he could come up with something to provide hope. Now remember, Krugel had relationships with the police, and in the past his machine had tracked dead bodies to a mortuary [which is where they normally end up], so it's not as though he didn't have *some* insider knowledge.

Insider knowledge + intuition = GPS tracking?

From shakedowntitle.com:

LANDMAN: *Watching his son asleep, Danie made a decision.*

KRUGEL: *I took a pair of scissors and cut off a piece of [his son's] hair… I worked until 5 o'clock the next morning. The first test… no result. Nothing worked. Then, from two metres, I could pick him up. The first positive test was two metres from where he was lying there on the bed. Then we started… 25 metres, 50 metres, 100 metres, then 50 kilometres and 150 kilometres. I believe that night – with Leigh Mathews – if I may say so, the Lord saw my heart.*

Quite amazing that over the course of a single night, Krugel built a GPS syncing DNA sampling tracking machine.

From shakedowntitle.com:

LANDMAN: *Carte Blanche put Danie to the test. We cut off a sample of our cameraman's hair and sent him to hide in a Bloemfontein cemetery with his camera rolling.*

Danie took two readings and within minutes [and perhaps a call from the local cops] he was able to point out where our cameraman was hiding. **The exact spot** *was pointed out on an aerial photograph...Hundreds, maybe even thousands, of people go missing around the world every day – often without a trace. But maybe not without leaving a few hairs on a jacket or on a pillow. Think of Osama Bin Laden, Lord Lucan or even Ananias Mathe – the man who'd escaped from C-Max. Imagine if their hair was available.*

In *Truth of the Lie* Amaral makes no bones about how the McCanns found out about Krugel. On television:

"[The McCanns] saw a television programme in which the effectiveness of Krugel's method was demonstrated, and so are persuaded that the man will be able to move the investigation forward. Without being convinced as to the validity of the method, the police end up acceding to their request..."

When Krugel touches down in Lisbon, he refuses to allow his device to be scanned or inspected at customs or security checks. Krugel won't allow it to be opened or x-rayed. Patents are apparently pending and the device's sensitive instrumentation can be damaged. Hours of negotiation follow, and Krugel eventually gets his way. Next stop, Faro airport.

Amaral is waiting for him there.

A Dodgy MO and a Gamechanging Breakthrough

"Krugel's machine leaves us all speechless [but] Kate and Gerry, they stick to their guns." — Goncalo Amaral's reference to Danie Krugel's arrival in Portugal, in mid-July 2007

"I feel betrayed. Eight months is one hell of a time to look for a child – to be told he is alive." —Varenda Gouws, a South African who employed Krugel in 2006

It is late on a Sunday afternoon [July 15th, 2007] when South Africa's inspector gadget, *Carte Blanche* producer Susan Puren and a mystery gizmo touch down in Faro. He's here, and she's here and his machine is here to track down Madeleine, to document the whole thing and maybe scoop up an award – or who knows, a patent – for their efforts.

Accompanied by Amaral, they drive to the Department in Portimao. In the building, on their way to meet a team of Polícia Judiciária investigators, they pass Amaral's office and Sofia's dead flowers hanging from a vase on his desk.

Krugel's opening gambit is to have the cops watch a video about his device. It's likely this was a recording of the *Secret Science Tested* episode from *Carte Blanche*, which had originally aired seven months earlier in South Africa. The producer responsible for the episode and Krugel suggest they simply watch and judge for themselves.

Oddly though, Krugel doesn't seem too keen on having cops examine the machine itself. He refers them to essentially a PR tape instead. Either way, the cops aren't convinced. The next day Krugel and a few cops head to Praia da Luz so he can kick off his magic act [although strangely, Krugel insists on only doing his measurements at night].

Now, months before Krugel wowed the Algarve with his hi-tech wizardry, he was tracking another super tough lead along South Africa's East Coast. I'm jumping out of the timeline briefly just to illustrate what the McCanns – knowingly or unknowingly – and the cops – wittingly or unwittingly – were letting themselves in for with this guy.

From shakedowntitle.com:

Varenda Gouws, 45, said Krugel led her and husband Willem on a wild goose chase after son Rayno, 20, went missing last year during a hiking holiday. [Gouws] gave Krugel a hair from Rayno's razor. He fed it into his Matter Orientation System, that he claims combines DNA testing and GPS-satellite technology to track down missing people anywhere in the world.

She said: "I can't say this machine doesn't work - but I know for a fact it didn't work for us." Rayno had last been seen taking a bus to Knysna in South Africa's Western Cape region.

True to form Krugel's gizmo seemed to hone in on somewhere close to where he was last seen.

From shakedowntitle.com:

Varenda said: "First Krugel told us Rayno was still in Knysna so we went to Knysna. Then he said he was in Port Elizabeth 150 miles away so we went to Port Elizabeth. Then he was in East London so we went there. Then he told us 'No, he's in the Transkei.' It was an endless track. We drove through South Africa for 4,300 miles. He absolutely convinced us saying 'Rayno is moving'. He said he must be in a truck or a car because he was moving so fast. Every time we left our jobs and packed up and went to these places and put articles in the newspapers. It cost us a fortune. But it's not the money, it's the mental torture. Being told your child is alright, he's moving around. We thought, 'Why doesn't he contact us?'"

Rayno's remains were eventually found eight months after he vanished in a forest outside Knysna. It is thought he died from a snake bite.

So, perhaps the original reading was right? What's interesting though is Krugel's response to being told, being confronted about having made a monumental mess in this case.

From shakedowntitle.com:

"It was clear that he had been dead for eight months because there was no flesh on the bones and there were ferns growing through the body. But when I phoned Danie to tell him, he was really aggressive. He said it was not possible. He blamed me. He said 'This is a lie. Nobody can tell you how long a body is dead'. He didn't want to hear he had made a mistake."

Of course, modern forensic science – real science – can reveal time of death with reasonable accuracy. Hair, curiously, is a key area where chemical tests can reveal a time-lapse for degradation/decay. This was used convincingly to determine the date of Helen Bailey's murder, and also, uniquely, that she was gradually and systematically poisoned.

Virtually the only remains of the unfortunate Bailey, dumped into a cesspool beneath her home, was her hair. Forensic toxicology found

Zopiclone traces in Bailey's hair; fluctuations in the dosages were used to calculate how long Bailey had been drugged, and if necessary, make projections as to when she died.

For all the McCanns' efforts to get Krugel to the Algarve, what's odd – frankly – is that they don't meet him at the airport, and the McCanns don't seem to be around when Krugel conducts his tests. The cops are once again looking for Madeleine and the McCanns are somewhere else – perhaps answering emails, or arranging the next press briefing.

Consider the scenario though. The McCanns were hanging around for weeks, ultimately for four months, to look for their daughter. They bring in someone from abroad and when he gets there…well, do they have other fish to fry?

In Kate's book, and in her diary, there appears to be very little on-the-ground detail, where they are out in the field, shoulder to shoulder with Krugel, trying to find Madeleine? But the Raven is out there. Even though the cops are far more doubtful than the McCanns about Krugel's dubious device, they're out there chasing leads. So, where are the McCanns? Wasn't this guy here because they had so much faith in his methods? So, where were they now that he was running around Praia da Luz?

From *The Truth of the Lie*:

Operations progress in the following manner.

1) *Krugel climbs to the highest point west of Praia da Luz, places a hair into the machine and traces an imaginary line in an easterly direction.*

2) *He repeats the operation to the north of Praia da Luz and traces another line towards the south.*

3) *He then determines the point of intersection of these two lines.*

4) From this point, he defines <u>a corridor about 300 metres wide,</u> <u>bound by the cliffs on the right and the Roman Baths on the left.</u>

Krugel then fingers a map and tells the cops, "Madeleine's body is in this area." Krugel's tricorder[46] had apparently homed in on Madeleine's DNA signal somewhere around the beach and the <u>Rocha Negra Cliff</u>. Krugel had done it again: he'd cracked the case.

He handed the cops an aerial photo of an 800-metre area. His machine had pinpointed Madeleine's precise location. It basically came down to one square kilometre mostly over a mountain range. It's difficult to say if this was an improvement on the original reading he'd made 12 000 kilometres away.

Naturally, the large area Krugel had identified had *already* been searched by <u>the National Guard</u>. Now, I don't mean to rain on Krugel's parade [well, I do…] but when I studied Praia da Luz for the first time, specifically the topography and terrain, it was hard to miss <u>those rugged</u> <u>cliffs</u>. Not to put too fine a point on it, but my first thought for dumping a dead body were those jagged black cliffs.[47]

Regardless, the <u>National Guard</u> [the ARG] are <u>called back to search</u> <u>it again</u>, but – as Amaral notes – "to no avail."

In Kate's narrative, dealing with May 4th, she refers to an anonymous neighbor directly across from their apartment coming over to report a car apparently 4x4ing in the night across the Rocha Negra volcanic cliffs. Kate specifically touches on "conjured visions of Madeleine being

---

46 The correct nomenclature for Krugel's patent pending tricorder is a "Matter Orientating System".

47 If the obvious place to search for Madeleine were the Rocha Negra Cliffs, then someone who seriously wished to conceal her remains would obviously not dispose of her there.

disposed of somewhere on the overhanging cliff." Doesn't that sound like someone imagining the little girl to be dead on day one?

And just three days after hitting Praia da Luz, before the jet lag even had time to wear off, Krugel's tricorder was pinging wildly towards… well…a mountain. It seemed vaguely disappointing that having been flown all that way [at someone's expense] the tricorder couldn't be *a little more specific*.

Despite the magic machine Madeleine was never found, and Krugel and the award-winning journalist returned from where they'd come, sans awards. History has certainly shown, that the most intuitive criminal investigator can be wrong, from time to time.

If this all seems much ado about nothing [and in a sense, it was] fate inexplicably chose *this* particularly part of the story to offer the investigation a black feather. Looking in the rear-view mirror, it's easy to miss this. So, let's slow it down slightly.

The first indication that something was stirring in the ether came from the McCanns themselves. Because in fact they had brokered Krugel's appearance in the Algarve and met him, if not while he was running amok, then just before he jetted back into the blue sky that brought him.

Let's rewind again and track back to how precisely the whole thing was arranged, when, how and by whom. It turns out that Gerry McCann called Krugel on June 9th and the two had a twelve-minute conversation. Krugel had apparently been recommended to the McCanns by email, hence the call. But other versions differ – some saying Krugel contacted the McCanns within days after Madeleine's disappearance. In Kate's book a friend of Krugel's begs her to give him a chance.

Initially they spurned his offer, so the story goes, but as the McCanns situation changed, and they had a chance to sleep on it, they apparently saw new merit in his services.

From shakedowntitle.com:

It is thought the McCanns initially welcomed Krugel's help – but have since changed their minds. A source close to Kate and Gerry, who gave Krugel a strand of Madeleine's hair after he flew to Portugal in July, said they are unconvinced by his claims and are keeping him "at arm's length".

Maybe so. But then why did they also keep Krugel at arm's length when he was in Portugal?

From shakedowntitle.com:

It is later said that whilst in Portugal, the McCanns effectively ignored Krugel, and when they finally met – before Krugel and Puren left – it was a very abrupt meeting in which the South Africans were 'made to feel like they were meeting Royals'.

Odd isn't it, the many layers to a single, silly little episode. It makes one wonder how many layers there are to all the other episodes?

From shakedowntitle.com:

Krugel, 42, contacted the family offering assistance two days after Madeleine disappeared on May 3rd. In July, Gerry allegedly rang him back to accept his offer after receiving a string of emails urging the family to use the South African. Krugel has told the Mirror his machine quickly traced Madeleine. He said: "I went to Praia da Luz in the middle of July and did the tests on Madeleine. I stayed there for four days, working at night time and all the data was the same. She was there in an area within walking distance of Praia da Luz but it is a very difficult area, with few houses. In my opinion the chances of her being alive are very, very slim."

Kate describes her reaction to the news that her daughter's DNA lay on the "Black Rock" mountain as a "final body blow". It's an incredibly strange choice of words, and she goes on to suggest that because Krugel's signal was located on rough terrain that had to mean Madeleine was dead.

It's a strange admission for July 2007 given the endless repetition in countless interviews subsequent to that period – on Oprah in 2009 and elsewhere – that the McCanns had [and one supposes would always] every reason to believe Madeleine was still alive. There was simply no evidence, or so the reasoning went, that she wasn't alive, so why go there?

Well, Krugel's entry into the game had two broad consequences. Firstly, I think the cops suddenly began to suspect the good doctors were not so good and not so smart after all. Their investment into Kruger's tricorder theory showed the doctors might have a screw loose themselves. If the ploy had been to show how easily the cops could be duped, and how dumb they were, it had backfired.

The second set of broad consequences were completely unexpected and came from Krugel – an ex-cop himself. And his apparently off-the-cuff comment as he walked out of the investigation would lead to the most effective undoing of his clients. Krugel's gamechanger came down to his suggestion that the Portuguese cops use sniffer dogs. Why not *actually* track Madeleine!

Implicit in this strategy wasn't so much the search for a missing living person, but the hidden remains of a dead one. It was a mental leap, not a huge one, but it was also just what the cops needed, and the McCanns had offered them the baton, if only indirectly.

Now, remember what had motivated Krugel to embark on the whole "locator" thing in the first place. It was the kidnapping and murder of Leigh Matthews. Krugel could see from miles away that none of that was in evidence here.

From shakedowntitle.com:

Krugel said he gave a copy of the map to Madeleine's parents and to the Portuguese police at the time, but refused to disclose details of his findings to the press for fear of anyone trying to disturb the scene. Now he wants to return to Praia da Luz to see if his equipment indicates that Madeleine's body is still there – or if it has been moved.

Asked whether he would like Krugel to return to search for Madeleine, Gerry McCann said he had no say in the matter.

"Kate and I have no control over who is allowed to go come and go into Portugal. This is a matter for the Portuguese authorities. Officially I cannot comment further, sorry."

If you read between the lines, the McCanns didn't publically involve themselves with Krugel, but did encourage both Krugel and the cops to work with one another, almost in a behind-the-scenes way.

This is a matter for the Portuguese authorities.

Kate and I have no control...

Except the McCanns were virtually in control of everything, in a sense, weren't they? The cops in Portugal were treating them with kid gloves, the media treated them as heroes [or cash cows] and Krugel?

A raven laughs overhead but when one looks into the blinding bowl of sky, there's nothing. Except...a black feather floating down. It all came down to a chance comment from the kookoo South African.

From shakedowntitle.com:

After his search, Krugel requested the Portuguese police to use sniffer dogs and a forensic team to search the area. "The sooner we find Madeleine's body, the sooner the police can find out who murdered her," [Krugel] said.

Up until then Amaral had been treating the whole thing the way he'd been told to treat it – by the McCanns. They were searching for a child that had been abducted. Well, what if they were searching the wrong way?

Ladies and gentlemen, my esteemed colleague...has just brought some new evidence to my attention...

But it wasn't just Krugel's circus act that jogged the Portuguese cops, clearly, it was also the McCanns themselves, and Kate, in particular. They knew about Kate's dream. Gerry McCann hadn't known about it initially but when he did find out about it he emphatically denied Kate had had any dream.

Krugel, in a sense, may have been brought in as dream damage control. Or possibly as an alternative premise to a dream. The goal appeared to be the same however, to sow the seed that Madeleine was dead even if her remains would never be found.

Two and a half months after her disappearance, the McCanns may have felt they wanted some sort of closure on the case, to move the narrative into the terrain of someone who'd died after being abducted so that they were justified in returning home and returning to work without her. Missing person's reports were coming out of the woodwork, and would they ever stop if Madeleine remained alive and missing? Each time there was one, were they really supposed to jump up and investigate? Krugel may have served the McCann's purpose potentially as a lightning rod for discussions beyond Madeleine as someone missing, but to usher in the prospect of Madeleine's remains.

The problem with this strategy – if that's what it was – was that Madeleine's remains had to *remain missing*. It was a matter of Madeleine becoming a missing dead person as opposed to a missing living person.

In the JonBenét Ramsey case, the Ransom Note has the same almost occult ability to conjure the little girl into and out of existence. Was she dead when the note was written [the Ransom Note referred to not returning JonBenét's remains for proper burial] or had the Ramseys indirectly killed their daughter by violating the terms of the note [not to contact police].

In any event, the cops investigating the McCann case had picked up an ominous but unmistakable change in tone.

From *The Truth of the Lie*:

It is at this time that, suddenly, the parents seem to admit the possibility of their daughter's death. Afterwards - and to this day, if I am not mistaken -, they take exception to this hypothesis. Perhaps we were being naive, but it had seemed to us that Kate was going to provide us, indirectly, with indications about where her daughter's body was to be found. Thus, at the beginning of June, she informed us that the body could have been hidden in the outlet of a sewer pipe at Praia da Luz, or on the cliffs to the west of the beach, where she happened to run. She will say later that this information had been given to her by mediums possessing psychic power.

Krugel seemed to snag onto the same intuitions, which is why he suggested sniffer dogs. And didn't it make sense to start sniffing at ground zero?

From shakedowntitle.com:

Krugel reportedly also first suggested that sniffer dogs be bought in to search the McCanns' apartment. It was the sniffer dogs' discovery of forensic evidence in the apartment that eventually led to Kate and Gerry.... being officially designated as suspects in the case.

Unfortunately for the McCanns though, there *was* evidence that Madeleine wasn't alive. There was blood evidence in their apartment and corpse smells tainting the Renault Scenic they'd hired 25 days after Madeleine's disappearance.[48]

---

48 Traces of Madeleine's blood was detected in the rear hatch area under the carpet of their hired Renault Scenic in the place of the wheel.

There was also a DNA match to Madeleine in the hire car and according to some, the DNA itself proved that Gerry was not Madeleine's biological father.

Sealing the Crime Scene [July 2007]

"If you bungle raising your children, I don't think whatever else you do matters very much."
— Jackie Kennedy

I mpossible as it sounds, after Krugel bugged out and <u>the McCanns did their dream damage control to the media</u>, the cops returned to apartment 5A, and sealed it off. It had stood empty for a month and then, one fine day the apartment was released and once again made available to a stampede of summering tourists.

Well, if the sniffer dogs were going to have a decent opportunity to do their thing, they were going to need the run of the joint. So, there was only one thing to do: 5A was going to have to revert to becoming a crime scene again.

From <u>shakedowntitle.com:</u> [This information was only released to the media in August 2008]:

The two-bedroom flat in Praia da Luz was crucial to the investigation with forensic teams dusting the shutters and specialists taking DNA samples from the furniture. It lay empty for a month after three-year-old Madeleine's disappearance, but was then available to tourists throughout the summer, raising fears of contamination.

Apartment 5A in the Ocean Club resort was eventually cordoned off in August after sniffer dogs from the UK – trained to detect corpses and human remains – were brought in. Their reaction prompted investigators to take further samples from the flat which were sent to the Forensic Science Service (FSS) in Birmingham for analysis.

Well, let's not jump the gun. Suspects love to trumpet "fears of contamination" in the media. Let's rewind a little and go through this part of the timeline step by step. For starters, the process of cordoning off 5A was initiated <u>not in August but July</u>, immediately after Krugel exited Portugal.

Amaral sounded the horn that they wanted sniffer dogs, and the South Yorkshire police answered.

From *The Truth of the Lie*:

Their dogs are specially trained to locate the most minute traces of blood and are capable of outstanding performance in the search for human remains and bodily fluids.

It starts with the South Yorkshire boys sending in their top man, a dude by the name of Mark Harrison. Harrison specialises not merely in missing person searches and natural disaster reconnaissance, but murder. He advises the British cops on a national basis and, unlike Krugel, has an impeccable and unimpeachable reputation at home and abroad. For these reasons and more, Harrison's arrival in the Algarve probably struck terror in the hearts of the McCanns.

If any traces of Madeleine were to be found, Harrison would likely find them.

From *The Truth of the Lie*:

It's July…We have to re-centre the investigation around its point of departure, apartment 5A at the Ocean Club, in Vila da Luz. We officially request the help of the best experts in criminology and forensics but also the specialist dog team from the English police. A few days later, we welcome Mark Harrison…

If the cops working with Krugel had been like mixing chalk with cheese, Harrison's entry into the investigation was more like adding a pea to a pod. It was a good fit.

From *The Truth of the Lie*:

He gets to work immediately, supported by the [Polícia Judiciária] and the investigators from Leicester and Scotland Yard. On his arrival, we place at his disposal details of the case, as well as all our material and human resources. Harrison reads up on the statements and interviews from the principal witnesses – including, of course, those of the parents and friends – all the analyses, simulations, hypotheses and cross-checking already carried out. He carries out a reconnaissance on the ground, by helicopter and then on foot. He paces the streets and the access roads to Vila da Luz and compares them to the diagrams created in the course of the investigation.

Now, if you think about it, it's interesting that Harrison's intense efforts are not reported feverishly in the media, even a year later. Try it yourself. Google Harrison's name and see if you find any details in the British mainstream media. [If you do, tweet them to me.] Instead, you will find Harrison's story coming up in Portuguese media.

How the British media glosses over this crucial area in the McCann narrative is telling; there's a bland catch-all theme running through the reportage [including the cited *Telegraph* article] that implies the apartment was contaminated and thus…why bother…could any effort really be conclusive?

One can almost feel the McCanns breathing over the reporter's shoulder. The investigation is undermined before it begins and yet… one must wonder…do the McCanns really want their daughter to be found?

From *The Truth of the Lie*:

[Harrison leaves] nothing...to chance: measurement and timing of possible routes between buildings, apartments and restaurants; analyses, with the help of the best specialists, of weather, geological and maritime factors in relation to the investigation; consultation with the best forensic anthropologist in the country, who indicates for us what would be the actual state of the body in the hypothesis of death occurring on May 3rd; study of the region's natural carrion predators. All the research already conducted by hundreds of people – GNR, civil defence, firemen and other volunteers – is re-examined in detail and re-analysed.

This guy is clearly someone who leaves no stone unturned. In other words, he's perfect to have on the McCann's team, assuming they really want to track down their daughter's remains. But did they? *Did they engage with Harrison?*

In Kate's book, Harrison's name comes up just three times, and one of those three instances is in the index as a reference to the other two. Sniffer dogs do faintly better in the McCann's account with six references, two of them in the index. To contextualise how dismissive this is, consider the fact that ice-cream is referred to six times [with no indexing], and Hubbard – the Anglican Minister who the McCanns confided in – makes around eleven appearances [two in the index].

So, it's safe to assume the McCanns didn't involve themselves in Harrison's deep drilling investigation either. We don't know what they knew, or even whether they knew Harrison was there, but one assumes if they cared about the investigation, if they went to the bother to hire an investigator from far flung South Africa, and if they were beating down Amaral's door every day for news of Madeleine, they *should* have known.

As things stood, on July 2<u>nd</u> the McCanns left the Ocean Club and rented a villa ["the cheapest we could find"] #27 Rua das Flores, in

Parque Luz. Kate describes it vaguely as a ten-minute walk from the Ocean Club. In fact, it was situated due West of the Ocean Club, and based on Google Maps, an undulating seventeen-minute walk.

The McCann's new digs were situated slightly behind a conical shaped hill. On the other side of that barren hill is the church, the beach, the Roman ruins and the town square. It's also a stone's throw from Rua da Escola Primária, the tunnel-like road sloping steeply down between canyon-like apartment blocks where the Smith sighting occurred.

Despite Kate's belief, and Krugel's for that matter, that Madeleine's remains are somewhere in the East, somewhere on the Rocha Negra, closer to Sir Clement Freud's mansion, the McCanns have located themselves further West, closer to a section of coastline that resembles a long and erratic scab. It's also the less busy and less scenic part of Praia da Luz.

Given Kate's dream two weeks after moving to the other side of town, it's possible the McCanns either wanted to be *further* from Madeleine's remains [with the implication that they were somewhere on the Black Rock], or they wanted people to think that's where Madeleine's remains were.

Consider the fact that the McCanns moved from 5A to the better views in 4G [including of 5A] after Madeleine disappeared. They didn't bug out of Praia da Luz or the Ocean Club for that matter because they wanted to stay close to Madeleine. Well, I believe the same held true when they moved to #27 Rua das Flores. I believe, and this is an early indication of what awaits in the final chapter, that Madeleine's body was initially hidden on the west side of Praia da Luz. If true, then the villa was closer to Madeleine's body than the Ocean Club.

Meanwhile, Harrison could hardly have been less interested in the Rocha Negra by the end of July.

From *The Truth of the Lie*:

After a week of intense work, Harrison presents the results of his study... his conclusions confirm our worst fears. ...there is no doubt that Madeleine is dead, and her body is hidden somewhere in the area around Praia da Luz...According to him, the time has come to redirect the searches in order to find... a body hidden in the surrounding area...

The main theme in the British account of this particular part of the narrative is about how the cops bungled the investigation by allowing 5A to be unsealed. It's an interesting ploy as narratives go, because had the police held onto 5A as a crime scene, that would have cast real shadows of suspicion over the McCanns, suggesting that the police felt they were involved.

Think about it. If your home is cordoned off and declared a crime scene on and on for months, what would the neighbours think? What would you tell your neighbours? Well, ditto a holiday apartment.

The British media seemed to play it both ways. Don't you dare suspect the McCanns. By the police not suspecting the McCanns [or at least, not suspecting there was something hidden or incriminating in their apartment, or in their wardrobe in their apartment, or behind the sofa in their apartment], they had also bungled their investigation.

The amazing thing is despite the stampede of summer flocks through 5A, and the likely flourishes of God knows how many housekeepers doing their cleaning in that apartments, despite the passage of almost three months, the sniffer dogs were still able to pick up the scent of death. That's amazing, no matter how you slice it.

From telegraph.co.uk:

The findings... suggest that traces of Madeleine's DNA were in the apartment and the hire car rented 25 days after she disappeared, played a large factor in making the McCanns suspects last September.

Although the couple, from Rothley in Leicestershire, have been cleared and the investigation closed, the apartment which played such a large part in the case still lies empty. The blunder was revealed in the extensive 30,000 page police dossier into the investigation.

Details of all those who stayed in 5A after the McCanns were disclosed in an internal document written by Chief Inspector Vitor Matos to Goncalo Amaral, who was then leading the investigation. It showed that the McCanns booked the flat from April 28 for a week, but moved out on the morning after Madeleine vanished on May 3 last year. They moved to neighbouring 4G with their other children, twins Sean and Amelie, and stayed there until July 3, when they moved to a villa in Praia da Luz.

The article goes on to describe the various visitors to pass through 5A. A retired teacher on June 12, a family of four from Falkirk in Scotland [who stayed almost two weeks], and then another couple from Hertfordshire. On July 19th, while Krugel had his game face on, a family of three pitched up from Leicester and like the McCanns initially planned, stayed for a week.

The police wanted to bug the McCann's apartment and their car, but a judge said he felt their statements would suffice. Reacting to the sniffer dog speculation…

From shakedowntitle.com:

The McCann family spokesman Clarence Mitchell said: "I think this particular revelation speaks for itself. We have always said that there were wholly explicable reasons for any material that was found. Kate and Gerry are as innocent today as they were on May 3 and if this number of people were in the apartment before the searches then I think people will draw their own conclusions about the strength of any material that was recovered."

What Mitchell perhaps didn't fully anticipate is that that is precisely what people did do; they started drawing their own conclusions and as they did the fail whale finally surfaced, blasting a jet of spray into the air as it did.

The Corner Interview [August 2007]

"We are living in a world today where lemonade is made from artificial flavors and furniture polish is made from real lemons." — Alfred Newman

I t's early August and the Raven is having dinner in scenic <u>Praia da Rocha</u>, by night a twinkling seaside playground on the southern fringe of Portimao.

The Raven is unusually nervous. He glances at his watch and sucks on a cigarette. Amaral knows "one of the most important search operations ever carried out in Portugal" is underway. Fates are hanging in the balance. And all he can do is wait. He draws on the cigarette turning the tip a bristling orange. Then sighing heavily, he exhales another plume of smoke into the warm summer air.

33.3km away, a grey jeep carries the dogs to the front of the building. Eddie's trainer, Martin Grime removes Eddie's leash and then impulsively, Eddie sprints off, right into 5A. Ill-discipline? Not a chance from a highly-trained sniffer dog. It's one of those grey areas – the removal of the leash also means "time to get to work", and Eddie, as if sensing the paralysis dogging *this* case of all cases, doggone it, wants to have a crack at it.

The trainer is immediately aware that Eddie is super-agitated. Eddie is scampering from the lounge to the bedroom and back again. He jumps onto a bed and then wheels back around. Eddie seems aware that *something* very bizarre is going on here. There's definitely *something* in the air, but for some reason it's just the slightest trace. Just the slightest whiff. It's here but…where? Eddie can't get a lock on it.

An investigator is standing by with a video camera, recording the entire scene. Grime calls Eddie back and tries to get the mutt settled and back on track. Precise orders given, Eddie turns and heads off. Now Eddie is sniffing the floor of the parents' bedroom.

Half an hour away by car, with the sea sighing soothingly over his shoulder, Amaral stubs out another cigarette. His friend asks him what he's so worried about. Amaral shakes his head then plucks out another cigarette. Beads of sweat form on the plucky detective's brow. He wipes it off but instantly new beads of sweat form. He lights up and then absently places the cigarette between his lips.

Elsewhere, and else when – perhaps earlier in the day, perhaps on a different day entirely [but still in early August] Kate McCann is resplendent in a green and yellow blouse. The Rocha Negra fills the background of their villa. She glances at her friend Jon Corner. Corner is a creative director at an advertising agency, and also a whiz with digital video production.

His camera glints at her. Speaking in a distinct Liverpudlian accent, Kate seems completely relaxed on a balmy summer's day in the Algarve. She says:

"It's not like there's a textbook about it; what to do when your daughter gets abducted…"

This was one of the first interviews I came across when I started investigating this case. I doubt whether I have seen Kate looking happier or more radiant on camera before or since. There's laughter. There are quips. The language itself sounds like someone on vacation, not a mother still grieving over an abducted daughter three months later. The lightness and levity of the scene, the brightness, is almost unbearable.

"It's funny we were on such good terms, like...we were all friends [touches her face] and the kids. And I think, because there's a group of us, you're just, you're into each other, do you know what I mean. Kind've... your interactions are with each other...So maybe if it was just me and Gerry and the kids. Erm, I mean he probably spends a bit more time looking round, you know. I mean we're all not used to this at all; and you know, it's horrible for anyone to have to go through. And we're just doing what we think's best. We don't know. You know, we don't know if what we're doing's right."

Eddie wanders over to the wardrobe and pokes his nose into it. Warm. He lifts his snout. Warmer. It's stronger here. Eddie wheels around, and does what he's trained to when he picks up an unambiguous signal: he barks loudly.

"<u>People say, 'How can he do that [give interviews].</u> How can he stand there and do that, when your daughter's been taken, and everything? <u>I mean, I've been like that before,</u> you know. And there've been other cases of kids that have been taken, and killed, or whatever..."

There's the smallest snarl of contempt in Kate's lip as she says the word "<u>taken</u>". Given the situation the McCanns are in in August and Kate's seemingly loosey goosey attitude to it on camera, one wonders what is *really* going on in her mind.

It's not like there's a textbook about it...

I will deal with the McCann's interesting reading material in more detail in a later narrative, but suffice it to say this is another possible match to the Ramsey case. The book *Mind Hunter* by John Douglas was spotted by several officers in the Ramsey home on the morning of December 26th, and eventually the allegation was floated that the Ramseys had used an FBI profiler's book as a "how-to-guide" to cover up and defeat the imminent investigation.

Well, the McCanns had strange technical manuals in their holiday library as well…According to Amaral, police who combed through the McCann's villa found Kate's side of the apartment filling up with photos of Madeleine in a sort of shrine. At Gerry's bedside – the man behind the blog and the fund - there was no such decoration. Instead, there was an interesting stack of books:

The Interpretation of Murder, by Jed Rubenfeld

Missing and Abducted Children: A Law-Enforcement Guide to Case Investigation and Program Management, National Center for Missing & Exploited Children;

Making Every Child Matter…Everywhere, CEOP (Serious Organised Crime Agency - Child Exploitation and Online Protection Centre).

And others. Amaral would note in The Truth of the Lie that:

"Mark Harrison himself wonders how Gerald McCann could have obtained these books…"

At 22:00, cops spy Gerry McCann driving in a hired Renault Scenic past their former apartment. Couldn't resist a look?

It's not like there's a textbook about it…

The very next day, August 2nd, at 18:00, the cops arrive at 27 Rue das Flores, the McCann's new villa, with Eddie and Keela, the cadaver dogs. They serve the McCanns with a search warrant and are surprised that the family, apparently expecting the visit, don't seem to object.

From *The Truth of the Lie:*

Eddie goes immediately to the lounge. He comes to a stop <u>in front of a</u> <u>wicker armchair on which is lying Madeleine's small pink soft toy</u> [Cuddle Cat], which <u>Kate was never without</u> in the <u>early days of the investigation</u>... Eddie barks to let us know that he has detected an odour: <u>the soft toy has</u> <u>been in contact with a [corpse]</u>.

Whether they knew it then or not, Eddie and the fraught yapping beside their wardrobe, yapping beside the wicker chair, yapping in the garden of 5A, yapping on the passenger side of the Scenic, had just become the stuff of the McCann's worst nightmares.

The Skye Interview [12 August 2007]

"We commit terrible crimes and we smile at the delight in getting away with it." —Pamela Meyer

On the night of Madeleine's disappearance *Sky News* was contacted using a computer borrowed from a retired British couple staying in an adjacent apartment. *Sky News* was alerted even before the Polícia Judiciária had left.

Exactly one hundred days later *Sky's* Amanda Walker sat down to interview the McCanns. It's not clear whether they're interviewed at the villa, or a somewhat non-descript hotel room which has the same basic set up as 5A. *Sky* pertinently captions the interview as taking place in a hotel, rather than a villa. It's unlikely that a freestanding house in the suburbs with a garden and a small pool would be mistaken for a hotel, right?

The couple appear seated and relaxed on blue couches similar to those in 5A, only in that they're blue. Behind them tissue-paper curtains, but not blue, billow through open windows.

Walker kicks off the interview with an excellent question. She asks the couple:

"Just take us through the emotional experience…"

Walker wants to know what it is like for the McCanns whenever there is a sighting of Madeleine given that then, as now, not a single sighting has been credible. Walker seems to add this detail – on the credibility of the sightings – slightly under her breath.

But let's rewind back a little and examine, word for word, Walker's first question to the McCanns. Let's get the full context. Bear in mind that a few minutes-walk from where they are sitting, their apartment has just been rebooted back to crime scene status and Gerry himself has been spotted driving near the apartment late at night.

Bear in mind too that Madeleine was supposedly abducted through an open window, and the McCanns sit down to the interview blissfully unbothered by the periodic poofing of the curtains behind them.

WALKER: *Over the past hundred days you have conducted a phenomenal awareness campaign. Which has led to various possible sightings...which have later been dismissed. Just take us through the emotional experience you go through from the moment that someone says 'I'm definite that I've seen Madeleine' to when it's discounted.*

KATE [Looking down]: *...I mean, the main thing for us is knowing whether the sighting is credible, really...[Pause]. To be honest, we don't go through that emotional rollercoaster...*

No, clearly not. But let's slow it down even further.

The McCanns *had* pulled off one coup after another in the media. If it wasn't the Pope[49] it was J.K Rowling [who herself lived in Portugal]. In August they were being wined and dined by a millionaire and were living like millionaires in a millionaire's mansion. They had gone from the grubby 5A ground floor apartment to the airy 4G and finally a plush

49 Within days of meeting the Pope references to the McCanns were removed from the Vatican website. [The content at the link provided from the *Mirror* has also been removed.]

villa with a garden and swimming pool. Their Find Madeleine Fund
was bursting at the seams [more on that later], their website's counters
were spinning as millions upon millions visited day in and day out, read
<u>Gerry's blogs</u> and made their donations. And so, when all these efforts
came to fruition and people responded – Madeleine *had* been sighted!
– how did the McCanns respond?

...I mean, the main thing for us is knowing whether the sighting is
credible, really...

But that wasn't really what the question was. The question was what
was the emotional experience around these sightings.

> To be honest, we don't go through that emotional
> rollercoaster...

But, why <u>wouldn't</u> you? Amaral has been chain smoking and chewing
his nails just at the thought of what sniffer dogs might come up with.
The McCanns on the other hand are very casual. They're interviewed in
shorts, <u>both wearing sneakers</u> and there are no emotional rollercoasters
in sight. Why not?

Why wouldn't you have your world turned upside down whenever
there was a sighting of Madeleine? Sure, by the time one saw a
photograph or went out to meet the missing child directly, by the time
the credibility of the sighting had been established one would expect a
simmering of emotions, and bitter disappointment. But there's none of
this here. In fact, there's very little actual following up leads – directly by
the McCanns – when it comes to sightings.[50]

---

50 Amaral's book has just five references to sight or sightings, including the
Smith sighting. Other references refer to "hindsight" and "not losing sight of
objectives", which is highlighted twice.

DOUBT

In Kate's book of the 40 references to "sightings", a quarter refer to books and generic terms and idioms such as "sights and sounds" and "line of sight" and "lose sight of" and ironically "out of sight out of mind." Another quarter refer to their friend Jane Tanner's sighting up the road, just behind apartment 5A on the night Madeleine was abducted.

The chapter "Key Sightings" rather than being shifted to the beginning of the narrative, it's <u>shafted</u> to the end, and here the remainder of the references stew. Most of them refer to two sightings made on the night of the abduction, namely Tanner's sighting and the Smith sighting. I will deal with both exhaustively in due course. But where are the dozens of other sightings? A page or two is provided as a sort of catch-all to go through six more sightings, which the McCanns were only aware of a year later in August 2008.

What were they doing in the meantime? And the tone is that the police negligently only provided them with these files months after the fact, and a few weeks before they closed the investigation.

Why not mention at the interview in August 2007 that the police weren't telling them about missing person reports? Well, I believe they were being told. Why wouldn't the police tell them? The police were reluctant to make the McCanns suspects, and if that were the case why wouldn't they communicate their knowledge of sighting to the McCanns? In fact, when one looks at Amaral's version of events it seems the McCanns were pushing sightings onto police desks and having the police follow every lead. It was as if the McCanns were putting the cops on a permanent rollercoaster ride so that they could wander around the fairground without a care in the world and really enjoy themselves.

"Fuck off. I'm ~~not~~ here to enjoy myself."

~ 157 ~

But the real insight into the *Sky* interview comes, I believe, even before Kate or Gerry answer the first question. It's a microexpression and easy to miss.

<u>Watch again.</u>

Now <u>watch the expression on Gerry's face</u> just as Amanda Walker says "<u>I'm definite I've seen Madeleine…</u>"

Many who have followed this case closely will be aware of this clip and the duping delight, but I want to take the issue further. Think about the words that are used that elicits a smile from Gerry. The words are: "I'm definite I've seen Madeleine…"

But in fact, the psychological seed Walker has sown was something else:

"Just take us through the emotional experience…"

One can see both Gerry and Kate are trying to plumb for the appropriate responses, the appropriate countenance, the right emotion for *Sky News*. Madeleine has been gone for one hundred days and this is about finding her, right?

Now, one would expect obvious grief, concern, longing and even desperation. One would expect some emotion. Anger, frustration, depression but grief above all. And yet none of it is there from either of them. What is there is a flicker, and yes, it's a flicker of emotion from Gerry. He's amused.

Kate looks down as Gerry smiles and then, as Kate begins to talk, Gerry glances at her, then he also looks down and then back up again. Now he has adjusted his bearing back to the appropriate sobriety and he immediately thinks of something credible to add to what Kate says.

When Gerry starts speaking his voice is very low and grave.

"I think it's a protection really, if you go up and down all the time... you wouldn't be able to function..."

The impression Gerry seems to be going for is that grief can make one so dysfunctional that it becomes impossible to function. An emotional paralysis, brought on by terrible grief, could kick in and lead to a sort of mental malaise and even depression.

Let's address these in turn. First the emotions and then the ability to function.

1. Blogs – Emotional Bankruptcy?

Now thanks to Gerry himself, we have a record of precisely how the McCanns spent their first fifty days. We know because Gerry blogged about it. So much for a mental malaise. When one converts the entire body of those blogs over the first fifty days to a 9000-word document, and one conducts various word searches for the various emotions, the results are sobering.

Happy: 9 matches.

"We are happy to support all strategies..."

"They were very happy that the director of ALGARVE Tourist Board...

"The Pope was happy to tell us..."

"...our first for TV and we were happy how they went..."

Enjoy: 4 matches.

Sad: 8 matches – all for the word "sad" inside the word ambassador.

So actually, not a single reference to the word "sad" or "sadness."

Incidentally Kate's book has 20 references to ambassador, 31 references to sad or sadness, and 41 references to happy.

In Gerry McCann's blogs over the first fifty days there's not a single mention of the words "unhappy" or "grief" or "mourning" or "longing". "Cry" is mentioned just once in the context of not knowing whether to laugh or cry about other children's messages to them.

"Feelings" is also mentioned just once, in the context of their feelings to the press when they met the Pope.

"Excited" is mentioned once, in reference to the Pope.

The word "missing" has thirteen references, twelve of them to Madeleine missing and only a single reference to "missing Madeleine terribly."

If one adds the positive emotions together there are around 14 references to positive emotions. In terms of negative emotions, there are only 2 references to grief.

2. Running and The Ability to Function

Roughly two weeks after Madeleine's disappearance [approximately May 20th], Gerry provides a blow by blow account of the family schedule. Amazingly it corresponds almost precisely to how the family were going through their routine before Madeleine's disappearance.

At 09:00 the kids are dropped off at Kids Club [as you do when there's been an abduction in the same resort]. Then the McCanns settle down to do PR, meet lawyers or the press. [Not the police however.] Interestingly computers aren't mentioned, even though the Find Madeleine Fund was a big priority early on and a big earner.

At midday, they pick up the twins and have lunch at the apartment. After 14:00 the kids are once again dropped off at Kids

Club and the McCanns then go for a run together, or go to church to say a prayer.

Then it's high tea with the kids and a brief tumble with them in the playground. The only major change is that the McCanns then cook dinner at home instead of heading down to the Tapas bar. The day ends with a prayer for Madeleine.

In all of Gerry's blogs, the word run features several times. If they were running regularly as a couple in some sort of routine, and it appears they were, there really doesn't seem to be any impairment in their ability to function. This intuition is reinforced, I think, in their interviews, where the McCanns, if anything, seem to need to remind themselves to be grave and to look grave and to try not to smile.

Taken, and killed, or whatever...

Phenomenal awareness campaign...

In the days and months that followed the Sky interview, some journalists started murmuring about the slick professionalism of the McCann's PR team. It wasn't just the Pope it was all the other celebrities too. Britain's entire football culture seemed to have rolled over to do their PR too.

For others, it wasn't mooching with celebrities that was disturbing as much as something far more basic: ordinary folk were beginning to feel Kate McCann's protracted failure in 2007 to shed a single tear – on or off camera – didn't quite look right. She just didn't look like a mother devastated by the loss of her child.

As for Gerry, as word of two sightings on the night of May 3rd filtered through the British media, some began to notice a common thread. Both mentioned that the man carrying the sleeping little girl with blonde hair <u>wore beige pants</u>...[51]

---

51 In some crime scene images of apartment 5A <u>a beige garment appears to be lying on the bed</u> in the adults bedroom. In <u>other images the beige garment has been removed</u>. It's also clear from these images that there was a second camera in the McCanns possession and that at the time of Madeleine's disappearance, <u>the clothes inside the adults bedroom wardrobe</u> [the shelves on the far left] had also been completely removed.

Auction for Kate's Diary?

"I always say, keep a diary and someday it'll keep you." — Mae West

K ate McCann, by her own account, hadn't kept a diary since she was a teenager. But at age 39, on May 4th, she started again. It was a lawyer's idea [a lawyer called "Hugh"] and the A4 notebook was Hugh's [no surname given] too. According to Kate, she didn't begin writing in earnest until May 23rd because for the first few days she was "an emotional wreck."

What's odd is Kate's diary doesn't start on May 23rd, or even May 4th, or May 3rd for that matter. It starts on April 28th. Kate says her purpose in keeping a record [which she admits she did consistently once she started] was "for the children." And also, it was therapeutic. And also, she could talk to Madeleine through her diary. And to God! And holy fuckamoly, she could even talk to the abductor through her diary!

I'm not sure how much of that is entirely accurate. Another possible reason to keep a diary is to keep track of everything. What she was saying and also her version of events. The diary could serve as a sort of reference tool to go to, to remember what happened. So, all the comings and goings could be nailed down there. You know, in case she started to forget what happened.

As I've said, Krugel is mentioned in Kate's diary, with a nice hedging around having no idea _at all_ how his gadget worked [yes, italicised and underlined], a note that it seems ridiculous but also the rationale behind it: _nothing_ [italicised and underlined] to lose. Well, thanks for that explanation, it might come in useful later [and perhaps that's exactly what Kate was counting on].

And sure enough, when Amaral got wind of Kate's diary, he wanted it.

From _The Truth of the Lie_:

We…wish to pick up the diary that Kate started to keep from May 3rd. Finally, we would like to question the group of friends again, to confront them about their contradictions concerning their system for checking the children during the evening dinners at the Ocean Club…

Amaral's also looking for more besides the diary. Where are the photos? More in particular, where are the photos of the couples taken at night? Amaral's trying to see who owns a pair of beige trousers and some photos taken at the same time Tannerman [AKA "Mr Khaki"] was spotted would be very useful.

From _The Truth of the Lie_:

We don't know what clothes the McCann couple and their friends were wearing on the evening of May 3rd…

Now, Kate had recently celebrated her 39th birthday [in April], so being on holiday a few days later there was likely to be some belated birthday partying. Last year in one's thirties before the roaring forties, and all that. So, where were the party pictures?

From _The Truth of the Lie_:

At the start of the investigation, we had requested all photos and videos from that day and from the other days, but **all we received were**

daytime photos; it was as if in the evenings and during the now famous
"Tapas," dinners, no photos had been taken despite the fact that some
of the diners had cameras with them. The lack of night time photos was
something we have never understood. Within the rogatory letter, we ask
the English authorities to seize photos and videos taken throughout the
holiday at the Ocean Club.

Is there any description of beige trousers in Kate's diary perhaps?
In her book, Kate mentions the colour "beige" just four times. It seems
she may have forgotten Gerry liked to wear beige, including in his first
television interviews while still in Praia da Luz. Would her diaries be of
more value?

One newspaper placed the actual value of the diary at £1 million in
September 2007.

From shakedowntitle.com:

*The diaries are currently in the possession of the Portuguese prosecutors
and there has been speculation that the document could even provide
forensic evidence. Meanwhile supporters of the McCanns see the seizure
as part of an intimidation of the missing girl's mother.*

But any potential value rests on the outcome of the police investigation.

*"The diary would chronicle the progress of the biggest human interest
story of the year, from an inside perspective," says [Neil] Denny [editor-in-
chief of The Bookseller magazine]*

*"So, if written well, and Kate McCann is an articulate woman, it could
fetch a significant sum, although I wouldn't want to put a figure on it. I
also would not be surprised if one of the journalists who has been on the
Algarve covering the case dashed out a book on the events so far. There are
certainly going to be plenty of books written about it in the future.*

Interestingly, when the Portuguese cops leaked aspects of the diary
to *News of the World*, Kate McCann said she felt "raped".

From shakedowntitle.com:

"This was totally out of the blue. It was Sunday lunchtime, we'd just got back from church and I got the text from Gail, who works in the nursery where Madeleine went. It just said, 'Saw your diary in the newspapers. Heartbreaking. I hope you're all right'.

"I had that horrible panicky feeling, confusion and, you know, what's she on about? I didn't have a clue." Kate said the story, printed in September 2008, showed *"absolutely no respect"* for her as she grieved. She added: *"I just couldn't believe the injustice.*

"I just recently read through my diary entries at that point in that week and I talk about climbing into a hole and not coming out because I just felt so worthless."

Somehow this seems like more emotion and indignation than when Madeleine disappeared, doesn't it? Now Kate is grieving? Now she's in a hole? Now there's injustice? Now it's heartbreaking and horrible?

Pardon me if this comes across as insensitive, but Kate's book had been published six months earlier,[52] and in it, Kate herself had inserted extracts from her diary. Six months also seems like the sort of period a publisher might stipulate for a tabloid to wait so that the public could absorb the original narrative.

Kate's insistence that the tabloid had published her words "out of the blue" and that she "didn't have a clue" don't resonate somehow. Would *News of the World* really take liberties and potentially need to dodge a libel bullet? Despite crying foul from the rooftops, it doesn't appear as though the McCanns sued *News of the World* nor even sought an apology, although they aggressively went after many other publications.

---

52 On May 12th, 2011, to coincide with Madeleine's birthday.

*One newspaper placed the value of the diary at £1 million in
September 2007...*

The other thing that <u>rings hollow</u> from Kate's statement is that her
notes on her daughter's disappearance automatically make *her* the
victim. And the real tragedy here is the cruel media. Kate feels worthless.
Kate feels disrespected. Kate feels there is no justice.

Knowing what we know thus far, <u>what about Madeleine?</u> All these
books, diaries and the tabloid frenzy turning like a hamster wheel with
Madeleine spinning in the centre. And who benefited from milking
rides month after month, year after year on the Madeleine Ferris wheel?
Talk about commoditising a crime instead of investigating it. Talk about
selling a crime rather than prosecuting it. Talk about pursuing all the
legal spinoffs to the crime rather than justice for the crime itself.

*...you have conducted a phenomenal awareness campaign...
which has led to various possible sightings...which have later
been dismissed...*

From <u>shakedowntitle.com</u>:

*John Blake...has published books on high-profile criminal cases...is
surprised [about]... interest in the diary.*

*"It would be **hideously insensitive** to make any advances at this
stage. But, of course, any publisher would want to get hold of the diaries.
Obviously, the ideal would be if Madeleine were found and the story had
a happy ending, in which case it would make a million-dollar book."*

In the end Madeleine was never found, but the diary documenting
Kate's anguish at her disappearance was serialised and made millions
anyway.

The September Dream Analysed

"The visionary lies to himself, the liar only to others." — Friedrich Nietzsche

When researching a cold case one needs to try to keep the time dimension alive. Looking in the rear-view mirror is safe, but it tends to allow small things and subtleties to recede into oblivion. In order to bring these disappearing specks back, one must systematically and slowly follow the timeline from the far side of history and carefully tick the various boxes as we come to them. Did this narrative mention this; why does that one leave it out? Is this mentioned in the police statements? Why is this in the media but not in the diary? Why is that in the book but not in the diary?

It's a laborious process and as such it's easy to forget the third dimension to true crime time travel – real time.

What does the present context reveal about the past?

If at turns some of this feels like a rehash of "Strange Dreams", bear with me. It's important that we pull the vital portent of Kate's "Turning Point" dream back into the narrative, and to do so again and again and again. When it comes to that dream, we need to rehash. It's difficult to over-emphasise just how big this stumble from the McCanns was, except to say it *directly led to them being seriously investigated as suspects.*

This may come as a surprise but it was only in early September 2007 – four whole months after Madeleine vanished – that the cops in Portugal announced the McCanns as suspects, and as such, were the subject of their investigation. What got the ball rolling was Kate's dream, Krugel's sniffer dog suggestion and the dogs themselves. But the announcement, that – gasp – the McCanns were prime suspects, is a dogleg waiting in the next chapter.

Now, coming back to timelines, rear-view mirrors and real time as contextual tools, let's re-contextualise the various narratives we need to juggle to interrogate the deeper portents hiding behind the "Turning Point" dream. Are there any?

In Kate's diary, there is zero mention of her having any dream about Madeleine in July, or any dream *at all*. That in and of itself is bizarre. I was a teenager when my mother died and I frequently dreamt disturbing dreams of my mother over a period of years. Why wouldn't one mention this most personal [but psychologically revealing] of experiences in a diary?

In Kate's book, she describes a pleasant dream in September in which Madeleine is alive and well. She pertinently notes that this is the *first time* she dreamt of Madeleine, and is seemingly bemused by the mysteriousness of the mind.

In Amaral's book, no mention is made of dreams of any kind either, besides this rather obtuse comment:

"It's July. The hypothesis of death, including by the parents, is being seriously considered…"

So, let's refresh our memories: where did the "turning point" dream come from again? If it's not in any of the core narratives then how did the media get hold of it? Did they simply conjure it for convenience sake?

The obvious answer is that in January 13th, 2010, two and a half years after Madeleine's disappearance, a year and a half after Amaral first published his book [and a year and a half prior to the publication of Kate McCann's book], the dream narrative emerged on the first trial day in a Portuguese court, in Lisbon. The source was a Ricardo Paiva, a Portuguese Police Inspector who acted as a liaison between the McCanns and the cops in the Algarve.

Paiva testified as follows:

"Kate called me, she was alone as Gerry was away and she was crying. She said she had dreamt that Madeleine was on a hill and that we should search for her there. [Kate] gave the impression that she thought [Madeleine] was dead – it was a turning point for us."

The "dream narrative", in other words, came to light like this:

1. Gerry flies to Washington on July 22nd, 2007 [returning July 25th, landing at Heathrow at 07:05 GMT].

2. While Gerry is away [July 22-25] Kate has a dream communicates to the cops that she's had a dream. [This is shortly after Krugel's hapless arrival, investigation and departure at the McCann's bequest].

3. Kate's dream implies two things: Madeleine is dead and her remains are on the Rocha Negra. [Krugel had also directed the police to search the same area – the East side of Praia da Luz].

4. Jump from July 2007 to January 2010. The McCanns try to suppress Amaral's book.

5. Gerry learns about Kate's dream apparently in court, appears angry and flustered in media interviews, denies that Kate had a dream, reiterates that they believe Madeleine is alive and shortly flies back to Britain without Kate.

6.   The "dream narrative" enters the media narrative.

Let's be explicit about this, the McCanns in 2007 [in Kate's diary], in 2010 [during the court case], in 2011 [in Kate's book] and to the present, don't wish to give the dream any airing. In Kate's diary, on July 18th, she notes:[53]

It was suggested that Madeleine is dead and buried in an area close to the beach, behind the cliff. What can I say?... I had a bad afternoon. I was very worried, desperate, extremely on edge. I don't think I can take any more of this, I really can't. How much longer will this suffering go on? I need Madeleine ALIVE.

It was suggested?

I had a bad afternoon.

I was very worried.

Extremely on edge.

I can't take any more of this.

How much longer will this suffering go on?

I believe there is a very good reason for this sudden uptick in Kate's anxiety in the last third of July. Concomitantly, I believe there's an excellent reason Gerry was so aggravated about Kate's contact with Paiva leaking into the court narrative, and from there bloodying the pages of British and Portuguese news media.

---

53 In Kate's book July 18th is emphasised as a juncture in the case, just as the diary emphasises the same thing. Interestingly the point is reinforced in the same sentence, describing July 23rd as the day "warning sirens" ought to have gone off. Immediately after this disclosure the narrative reverts to Gerry's trip to Washington, leaving Kate alone and in a sort of panic mode.

What does this mean?

I need Madeleine ALIVE.

Why is Kate wanting Madeleine alive on July 18th of all days? Why does Madeleine being alive on that day matter as opposed to say, any other day?

Part of the answer comes via our knowledge not only of what the sniffer dogs zeroed in on, but also – and far more particularly – *when* they did. It's important to note that the casing of the McCann's original apartment [commencing on July 31st] and the testing of the vehicle [August 6th] and the various clothing and apartment deployments [August 1st – August 8th] didn't happen on the same day.

To recap, the "dream narrative" came about as a result of the McCann's attempt to have Amaral's book banned. The parties sparred in court, and Ricardo Paiva gave evidence of a telephone call made by Kate, while Gerry was absent. He said that Mrs McCann told him in a tearful telephone conversation in late July 2007 that she had dreamt that Madeleine was on a hill and that police should search for her there.

Kate's book, published a year and a half after these revelations, unsurprisingly refers to her phone call to Paiva possibly on the night of Gerry's departure to Washington. The narrative is different however. According to Kate, she called Paiva on the premise of simply wanting letters translated. Paiva then sort of unloaded onto Kate. Paiva sounded "distant". Paiva sounded "strange". In Kate's version of events, Paiva "wasn't his usual self" rather than Kate herself.

Krugel had convinced the cops to change direction. This is the implementation, I think, of the ploy I touched on earlier. Which is, you bring in Krugel to discredit the cops. You have them work together and then try to turn them both into a laughing stock. It's a ploy to discredit.

As Kate puts, surely the cops weren't placing "too much faith in the findings of an unknown and untested magic machine?" Of course, they weren't, but kudos for sowing the seed. At the critical juncture, Krugel is the mastermind behind the turn in the investigation.

Of course, there's a glimmer of truth in that, but what's missing is Kate's admission of her own involvement not just in recruiting the "ridiculous" Mr. Gadget but also in what she *actually* said to Paiva.

Despite all these problems the biggest problem for me lies within the seemingly pointless narration of Kate's September dream. That may seem like overstating things – how or why would a mere dream have any bearing on the investigation. Well, psychology in true crime is huge. The psychology here, the invoking of dreams is where the shit becomes real.

So, what happens in the dream that's so significant? Well, very little happens in the dream besides the fact that Kate *remembers* Madeleine apparently for the first time in months. In a sense the September dream is a sort of un-writing of the dream narrative that emerged in court, and then re-scripting it in more positive terms.

Did you hear Kate had a dream about a hill? No, I only know she dreamt Madeleine was still alive and at kindergarten, safe and sound. Oh, I must have got your wires crossed. Must be, it's in their book and it's lovely, Madeleine reappearing like a little angel…

What matters here isn't so much the dream itself, which for me lacks the ring of truth. What matters is the residual psychological code that is inadvertently embedded in the dream. It's a little like the mind leaving psychological DNA even in a deliberate attempt to malinger. Yes, the mind works in mysterious ways.

Here's what I mean, and yes, looking in the rear-view mirror it's easy to miss the obvious:

If Kate swoons over her angelic child, Madeleine in Kate's off-kilter dream *doesn't seem to remember Kate.*

In the September dream, though Gerry is *implied* being present, he's never mentioned either, nor the twins.

They're there and yet absent, and the Madeleine apparition never acknowledges her father or her siblings.

But neither – and this is crucial – **does Madeleine acknowledge her mother** even in her mother's reframing of it.

In the September dream Kate runs over to Madeleine and luxuriates in Madeleine's warmth and light [whatever that means].[54] Kate repeats that she "held" Madeleine three times.

Madeleine also holds Kate, but that's all she does. Holds not hugs. There are no words, no movement from Madeleine [because she's dead]. And yet she *holds.*

---

54 Was Madeleine's "warmth and light" and the idea of "luxuriating" psychological code for the treasure that flowed through the publicity Madeleine garnered for the McCanns?

Time to Duck

"Being stuck in airports, you always end up buying perfume and sunglasses." — Lexa Doig

Because of Madeleine's disappearance the entire McCann family were stuck in the Algarve for four months longer than they meant to be. They were all effectively *being held*. Their lives were *on hold*. And Madeleine, one way or another, was the force field at the centre of it.

We must take the September dream symbology even further. Kate held [seized] Madeleine and Madeleine was held and held and held until she became a *means*. The McCanns seized the *story* of their daughter and spun it into gold. Does that make sense? And though the McCanns didn't realise it initially, Madeleine – not their daughter but a dissolute phantom and perhaps a phantom of their own making – was also holding *them* together in a vice-like grip.

I will elaborate on what may seem a flimsy point – that Madeleine *held* the McCanns – in due course. I do want to sow the seed right now of Madeleine's body being placed somewhere by someone in Praia da Luz. More than three weeks later the cadaver scent manages to cling to the outside of a seven-seater rental, albeit along the inset along the lower trim of the passenger door.

As a rental, <u>many people sat in that car</u> prior to the McCanns' use of it from May 27th onwards, and even during the rental period, various people besides the McCanns made use of it. There were trips to the beach, trips to the airport, trips to buy groceries. Sometime in July, sometime after the McCanns had moved into the villa behind the hill, a neighbour happened to notice <u>the rear hatch of the vehicle standing open all the time</u>. As if the McCanns were trying to ventilate the vehicle. As if they were trying to get rid of a bad odour.

It must be noted that <u>the driveway to the villa is long and fairly secluded</u>, so not just anyone <u>would see the vehicle</u> or what was going on in and around it [which was perhaps the point].

Michael Wright, identified as a second designated driver <u>on the credit card contract</u>, also remarked on this odour, and attributed it to the twin's nappies and garbage bags stewing in the back of the car. <u>Sandy Cameron</u>, Gerry's brother in law, provided this version for the source of the smell:

"On one occasion, I believe it was on July of 2007, I took Patricia[55] *to the supermarket. We carried bags in the boot (trunk) of the Renault Scenic; bought various items including fresh fish, shrimp and beef...After this shopping trip and still in the month of July 2007, I began to notice a strange odour in the car...we removed the carpet from the boot (trunk) in order to clean it. I tossed (beat) the boot carpet* **to remove any particles** *and cleaned it with a wet cloth and left it to air out."*

There's much more to drill down to, but we'll get to it in due course.

In <u>August, Martin Grimes</u>, a FBI Specialist Advisor in canine forensics [the dog handler in other wards], submitted his [rather damning] report to the Portuguese authorities.

---

55 Trish Cameron, Gerry McCann's sister.

Near the end of the same month, Michael Wright returned to Praia da Luz. Staying for around ten days, Michael booked a removal firm in Lagos using his own name. This is indicative that the McCanns were already angling to return to England in August. So, what changed for them in August?

On the last day of August, the McCanns launched a libel action against *Tal & Qual*, a Portuguese newspaper. The paper claimed the "police believed" the McCanns had killed their daughter. The McCanns shouted from the rooftops how "deeply hurt" they were by the allegations against them.

Meanwhile, back in Birmingham a forensics lab had found matches to Madeleine's DNA taken from a sample from the Renault's boot [tyre compartment]. Fifteen of nineteen components checked out. The lab deemed this result "too complex for meaningful interpretation."

In fact, almost every sample checked came back with the same news:

"No confirmed DNA of Madeleine McCann in any of the tested areas of interest in Apartment 5A..."

Had washing and cleaning efforts and the passage of time degraded what little traces Madeleine had left of herself?

It seemed the sniffer dogs were more effective than the actual lab at microanalysis, unless the sniffer dogs were having an unusually off day. Well, perhaps the lab was too.[56]

Irrespective, on September 7th, the portents published in *Tal & Qual* proved to have some basis, if not in fact then in the intentions of the cops. The McCanns were declared arguidos at last, but not before both Gerry

---

56 The government run FSS lab that tested the McCanns/sniffer DNA was eventually shuttered in March 2012 after running monthly losses of up to £2 million.

and Kate were hauled in for a final session of gruelling questioning. They were asked to account for the sniffer dog evidence. Could they?

I'll deal with that in a subsequent narrative. In any event, just two days later the McCanns duck out of the Algarve. They drive to the airport in the same Renault Scenic they've been driving all along. On September 9th, their white and orange EasyJet taxis onto a runway and the McCanns emerge to the whirs and clicks of a gaggle of ravenous reporters. The headlines in England are less than welcoming. The *Daily Express* blasts their arrival with:

"WE CAN PROVE PARENTS DID IT"

As Gerry descends the jet ladder, something very strange happens. A black fire appears on the ground and takes the shape of a raven. And then the raven that doesn't belong flitters closer to where the McCanns are stepping down, out of the jet.

Somewhere across Britain and Ireland,[57] fates align and a certain Mr. Smith turns on his television and sees Gerry emerging, descending the steps. The blonde-haired child in his arms is dead to the world, and the way Gerry is holding Sean, and the way Gerry seems to avoid looking directly at the cameras, sparks something. Mr. Smith is certain he's seen this man before, on the night of May 3rd, in Praia da Luz, moving quickly, carrying a little girl with blonde hair in the direction of the beach.

And with that a gigantic black wing flashes across the sun.

---

57 Likely Drogheda, one of the oldest towns in Ireland.

SHADOWS OF DOUBT

"To think of shadows is a serious thing."
— Victor Hugo

The Blackbird Pie UnBaked

"Wasn't that a dainty dish, To set before the king..."
— Tommy Thumb's Pretty Song Book, 1744

Blackness. The back and forth crush of the sea along slabs of slanted rock. The black wing shifts. The jagged, feathery edge reveals no more than a broken silhouette, the dark Western fringe of Praia da Luz.

Above the sky is starless. To the East is the black hulk of the Rocha Negra, only visible because the beach below it is an almost imperceptible shade lighter, and a far-off line of coast-hugging lights is broken by its bulk. On this side, along the tiny coastal corridors that pass for one-way roads, a few veranda lights burn through the night. The dull, sodium light burning for hours on end flies ambitiously over the coastal shelf. It gets no further and does no better than to tint the nearest foams as they coarse closer with the tides.

Although impossible to see, the raven is here. It moves stealthily over the rocks, walking, hopping, occasionally flapping over a slippery section or a protruding plank.

Madeleine, of course.

Where is she?

She was...here.

<u>But how do you know?</u>

The raven doesn't answer. Casting around in the murk, it's difficult to get one's bearings here. Where exactly *is* here? And what is that smell?

Still, the raven doesn't answer. The quality of the light however, seems to change. Imperceptible at first, the dawn begins with the coldest moment of the day. In the same way, just before the dawn the far horizon seems to become darker than ever. And that darkness is here, on the West side of Praia da Luz.

The raven remains invisible in the inky blackness, black on the glistening black-brown of the rocks, black with the infernal black ocean sinking into the limitless night. Though one cannot see it, sometimes when the sea pauses, one can hear its feet scraping against stone.

<u>How do you know?</u>

There's nothing to see, nothing to guide us except this sound which gets lost and found in the ebb and flow of the ocean. Tracking it one turns and then even the sound is lost.

She was...here.

Madeleine? Madeleine was here?

Madeleine, of course.

Where is she?

Where is her mother?

And suddenly, there she is. A ghostly apparition to be sure. The silver form of a slim woman with silver hair clutching a strange child's toy in the dark is unmistakable. These are <u>her rocks</u>, she will say, and she will come here again and again, alone, to grieve. And now, here she is, a spectre in a dream.

She moves closer, close enough to see the brand on her ghost shoes.

Where is she going?

Madeleine, of course.

The raven follows and so, so must we. The ghost steps over the rocks, free from the laws of physics but not, apparently, the Earth's gravity. The strangest thing is the expression on the ghost's face. There are no tears or prayers. There is no grieving. Instead there is a frown. Intelligent eyes scan back and forth and then the spectre walks further.

What is that smell?

And the ghost appears to sniff the air too, and then vanishes.

Another dreamer intrudes, though not as a ghost. His thoughts taint the ether, sleepless thoughts in sleepless dreams. There is a faint static to them, which is like poison to its antithesis.

The raven starts from a rock and perches on our shoulder.

Don't look, listen.

From shakedowntitle.com:[58]

...He has not slept and is worried sick. He states he was watching the 10 pm news on BBC and saw the McCanns getting off the plane and coming down the steps. He states it was like watching an action replay of the night he saw the male carrying the child back in Portugal. He states the way Gerry was carrying his twin triggered something in his head. It

---

58 The statement made by Martin Smith in Ireland is signed by Kate's liaison with the police in Portugal, Inspector Ricardo Paiva, and dated 27 September 2007. Smith and his family had first reported the sighting [of a man carrying a child and subsequently known as the "Smith sighting"] at the police station in Portimão on the morning of May 26th, 2007 at 10:40.

was exactly the same way and look of the other male seen the night Maddy went missing. He also watched ITV news and SKY news and inferred it looked like the same person both times carrying the children.... He was with a group of 9 family and friends the night he saw the male in Portugal. He sounded quite shaken and worried whilst speaking to me.

Don't listen, sniff.

What is that smell?

It is the same smell on the trim of the Renault. And this, perhaps, was the prime problem they faced. Not to hide from sight, though there is that, but how to hide a smell for weeks on end knowing a stampede of summer flocks was on its way to the Algarve.

On the 17th of September, just ten days after being officially announced as suspects, and barely a week following their arrival home in Rothley, the McCanns sought to find a legal way to deal with the sniffer dog scent bedevilling their credibility.

From telegraph.co.uk:

Kate and Gerry McCann's legal team has contacted American lawyers over a case where key sniffer dog evidence was thrown out of court in the hope that it may help them fight any charges that they were involved in the killing of their daughter. Their UK lawyers consulted the legal team of Eugene Zapata, 68, who is accused of murdering his estranged wife Jeanette in 1976.

He was charged with murder last year after dogs indicated that they sniffed human remains in the basement of the former family home in Madison, Wisconsin. But a judge ruled last month that the evidence was no more reliable than "the flip of a coin" and could not be put before a jury.

At the same time they were trying to dodge the sniffer dogs, the McCanns launched a new media campaign [including in Spain] and received a large cash contribution and insight from an unexpected source.

From shakedowntitle.com:

In the last 10 days they have been declared formal suspects, accused of fleeing Portugal and endured a number of slurs about their parenting but they began to fight back by launching a newspaper and poster campaign focused in Spain and Portugal to highlight Madeleine's disappearance.

The couple were also boosted by the public backing of Sir Richard Branson, the Virgin boss, who contributed £100,000 to kick start a fund to pay for their legal team. [Branson] has taken a personal interest in the investigation and has spoken at length to Mr and Mrs McCann...

Why on Earth are there all these problems around one simple couple, and one simple case?

Why on Earth are there all these problems around a simple photograph?

Where on Earth are Madeleine's remains?

The mystery seems impenetrable until we look through the true crime looking glass into a reference case.[59] Similarly inexplicable impasses seemingly haunt the unsolved JonBenét Ramsey case. Beneath the gossamer, we discovered a silver star – that of Lockheed Martin, one of the world's largest companies. Lurking just beneath the silky surface

---

59 This narrative is not the first to draw a link between the unsolved mystery of Madeleine McCann's disappearance and the unsolved Ramsey case. From guardian.com: *"The original [Panorama] film would have compared Madeleine to the JonBenét Ramsey case in Colorado..."*

of the Ramsey case were enormous piles of treasure. Treasure that could be lost but not if some interlocutor could be found, or *conjured*.

And thus, the cold Christmassy mystery of the Ramsey case begins and ends with the Ramsey Ransom Note.[60] No kidnapper ever called, so the note itself became a dead end. It became "evidence" leading through a doorway of infinite possibilities but nothing definite [beyond possibilities of disguised handwriting].

The same gossamer obscures the McCann case, and crazy as it sounds, it is the gossamer surrounding a single digital image and an obscure piece of coastline.

1. The "Last Photo" Reveals itself.

The missing child image chosen for Madeleine has the same quality as the bogus Ransom Note. The obscure piece of coastline, I believe, has the same quality as the basement at the extremity of the Ramsey home.

The Ramsey kidnapping note ["there's a note here and our daughter's gone"] presents a bogus image in the sense that no child is missing, certainly not a living child. When we apply this to the McCann case, if no child is actually missing then there's also no need to have *an up to date image*. Do you see?

Buried in the bogus narrative is *another* narrative. And in this narrative, it becomes *secondary* to have an image perform its original function. As such, and this is a test of the subterranean narrative, the image needs to perform *some other function*…such as…?

---

60 The same question can be asked of the Ramsey Ransom Note. Why go to the bother of penning a three-page note, disguising handwriting, all this at tremendous risk to the author/authors? The answer is more straightforward than one might imagine: because the stakes were extremely high. Careers and fortunes stood to be gained or lost. A family [and perhaps several] could be literally devastated if custody was removed.

Don't look, listen.

Don't listen, sniff.

What other function could an image for a missing person – who isn't really missing – possibly have?

...tug at the heartstrings....

Which image would inspire you to donate money [or at a minimum, play on your sympathies]:

<u>This one</u> or <u>this one</u>?

And if you were the police trying to get the public to find a genuinely missing three-year-old:

<u>This one</u> or <u>this one</u>?[61]

In a real sense the "last photo" gives us incredible psychological insight into this case. Already we can see plenty of unnecessary and distracting noise "clouding" the image, and as we're about to see, <u>what the image itself purports to be</u> appears to be a deliberate misdirection. If there's been mischief with the timeline of the last photo, <u>what further mischief lies in store</u> when the timeline *really* matters?

2. Lifting the veil from the Rocky Coast

The raven shifts on our shoulder. Well, the spectre that was there is gone. But there does seem to be the slightest bit of light now.

---

61 <u>The "pool area" background of the image</u> indicates it was definitely taken during the family holiday. The <u>clothing appears to match</u> what <u>Madeleine wore onto the plane</u> when they departed the <u>East Midlands Airport</u>. Note the overcast conditions.

We make our way over slanted slabs, passing the moon grey fisherman's huts one by one, stepping, trying not to stumble but stumbling anyway. Where was the spectre going? Was it here? Or by these tall bushes?

Don't look, listen.

But what about the spectre?

Don't listen, sniff.

But where…where was she going?

Madeleine, of course.

We walk a little further, the raven's wings opening as we hop and teeter across the rough and soapy rocks. And then, there they are. Half moon coffins beached on the beach and a smell like an open sewer spilling into the sea.

~

Exit Goncalo... [October 2007]

"Justice is done in silence."
—Mantra of the Polícia Judiciária

When the McCanns produce a report that invalidates the work of the sniffer dogs ["without a body the canine search can't be confirmed or definitely proved"] Goncalo Amaral's blood begins to boil. Assuming the FSS in Birmingham had a hand in it, Amaral is speechless. How *else* did they get hold of confidential information?

The Raven lights a cigarette and ruminates. The words of the McCanns percolate painfully through his head, like the crow of a rooster over a sleeping town.

"Find the body, detective, and prove that Madeleine is dead..."

Amaral knows the counter is just as valid. If she is alive, where is she? Of course, in circumstances like this, fortune seems to favour the defendant. The burden of proof is on Amaral and his team, and the fact is, there's very little. So much is covered by darkness.

From *The Truth of the Lie*:

During the night of Saturday into Sunday, our dog does not stop barking. I go out but I see nothing and nobody that could get him so worked up. He then howls by the door. I don't know what's going on, but being on my own with Inès, I decide to stay close to her indoors and not let my anxiety show. The next day, I still don't understand what could have upset the dog so much.

And so, a thorn begins to wedge itself in the detective's side. A thorn born of anxiety and yes, anger. Back at work he has to deal with countless reports of sightings. One, emailed from Buckingham Palace. Another from an English tourist called Kate who saw someone strange at the supermarket near the Ocean Club.

But the Raven must chase every phantom, and so he hangs up his hat, and with a sigh, sits down and gets to work.

From *The Truth of the Lie*:

In the evening, while driving, I receive an unidentified phone call, the last straw...A journalist asks me if I want to comment on the subject of the email. Whether due to the difficult day, the raging storm or the fact of driving through rain...I lose my cool. I reply, irritably, without thinking, that the message is of no interest and that it would be better for the English police to occupy themselves with the Portuguese investigation.

Even as he ends the call, Amaral knows he's in trouble. The journalist, unsurprisingly, pounces on Amaral's pique and in short shrift, the ball is in the other court. Amaral knows what he faces: *not being able to continue to direct the Portimão Department of Criminal Investigation.*

When Amaral arrives home he finds out what has gotten the dog riled up so much. His neighbour's home has been burgled. But there's something sinister about the burglary. Valuables aren't taken. They seize only a briefcase filled with notes. Amaral lights another cigarette.

Did they mistake their target?

The storm continues to pound the Algarve with rain. The detective heads off to Huelva in Spain for a work function. When Amaral picks up a newspaper to read on the way there he sees his own words shouting back at him on the front page. Later that day the Raven listens to a bishop intoning about cops and their mandate to protect the rights of children.

He visits the monastery where Christopher Columbus stayed while waiting for the backing of his Queen. When he got it, he sailed into history, and a New World.

But the fates are not so kind, not today, for the detective. British television had just aired commentary on the lack of professionalism by Portuguese police the previous night, and as he feared, Amaral's pique entered the post-broadcast discussion. The rumor mill churns and Amaral's words are recycled and escalated until it becomes "an incident".

From *The Truth of the Lie*:

... shortly after 2pm, in the middle of lunch...I receive the news. The National Director has sent a fax to the Portimão DIC: in it, he stipulates the end of my assignment and requests my return to Faro. Today, October 2nd, is my 48th birthday; this is not the present I wanted, but one that I was expecting. Basically, this brings to an end a campaign of defamation and insults that I have been the target of since the start of the case, the whole thing orchestrated and amplified by the British media.

Their strategy had been straightforward. To discredit Portugal as a Third-World nation, and do the same to its prosecutors and police force.

From *The Truth of the Lie*:

According to a British correspondent, the Prime Minister [Gordon Brown] personally called...to ask for confirmation of my dismissal.

Why would the head of the British government be interested in a lowly Portuguese official?

Rumours abound that the British want Amaral's head as part of a list of demands for becoming signatories to the Treaty of Lisbon.[62]

From shakedowntitle.com:

The Treaty for the first time gave member states [like Britain] the explicit legal right to leave the EU and the procedure to do so...The signing of the Treaty of Lisbon took place in Lisbon, Portugal on 13 December 2007. The Government of Portugal, by virtue of holding Presidency of the Council of the European Union at the time, arranged a ceremony inside the 15th century Jerónimos Monastery, the same place Portugal's treaty of accession to the European Union (EU) was signed in 1985...[However] Prime Minister Gordon Brown of the United Kingdom did not take part in the main ceremony, and instead signed the treaty separately a number of hours after the other delegates. [Brown cited needing to]... appear before a committee of British MPs... as the reason for his ~~snub~~ *absence.*

Madeleine, of course.

Well, for some reason Brown wasn't happy with the Portuguese, or the treaty, and the McCann case certainly played into that bristling discontent.

What nobody expected, not even the Raven himself, was the boon his dismissal from the case would bring. It allowed the 27-year career detective to look at the case dispassionately, but it also allowed another door to creak open. As a cop secrecy laws barred Amaral from breathing a word about the case, and out of everyone involved, Amaral had a lot to

---

62 The Treaty of Lisbon, signed in December 2007, amended the Maastricht Treaty of 1993. It has subsequently been referred to as the Treaty on European Union [2007].

say. There was no way he was going to walk out of his career with this – this *humilhação*[63]– hanging over him.

And gradually, through the ether, the tide reached out and offered the Raven an olive branch. While the official case languished in inertia, something big and white was moving through the doldrums. The fail whale…

From *The Truth of the Lie*:

…when I left the Criminal Investigation Department in Portimão, in October 2007, nothing was known about this vehicle, about this issue of the open car boot. We knew that inside the vehicle cadaver odour and bodily fluids had been found, where Madeleine McCann's DNA profile was extracted from, with 15 alleles. Months later, there is a jurist, who lives nearby, who came to report that after the McCanns arrived at this villa, they saw the car boot open from then on…

It was exactly the spark the Raven needed to get back into this case, not as a cop, but as someone who simply wanted to know the truth. Had a concerted effort been made to mislead?

---

63 Humiliation.

The Tanner Ruckus (November 2007)

"Doubt is not a pleasant condition, but certainty is absurd." — Voltaire

Jane Tanner, one of the Tapas Seven, was a 36-year-old marketing manager at the time of Madeleine's disappearance. Amaral describes her variously as "adamant" and "extremely sure of herself."

Tanner's eye-witness account would certainly prove to be a curse seemingly without end for one Robert Murat, a bespectacled British chap who could speak Portuguese and who – unusually – lived in a house on the projected route "Mr. Khaki" seemed to be taking. Thanks to Tanner and the McCanns themselves, Murat had the pleasure of becoming the first official suspect in the McCann investigation.

More than 500 individual apartments were searched along Mr. Khaki's projected route as well as Murat's home. The sniffer dogs were sent to his home as well, and allowed to sniff his vehicle with zero results. Yet Tanner, while sitting in a tinted vehicle, insisted Murat was her man.

Because Murat ultimately turned out to be a bogus lead, he was cleared in September 2007, I won't be going down the Murat alleyway in this narrative. So why deal with the Tanner ruckus at all? Firstly, Murat falling off the suspect cart didn't help the McCanns, especially since they were replaced as prime suspects. Perhaps not surprisingly, just two months after Murat was cleared a new alternative suspect was conjured. It came through Jane Tanner's testimony, and since she'd never described a face in her original identikit, she could theoretically fill in the blank with someone else.

Did she do that? That's what we want to find out. Was there more going on than that, not just with Tanner, but with the others? Ditto the McCanns. In the next narrative, I'll be dealing with the Tapas seven in far greater detail as well as the inconsistencies between them and the McCanns.

What we want to test here and as we push on through this decade-long saga, is whether there was an integrated effort to mislead. If there was how concerted was the effort to mislead? How many people were involved? Who was involved? If they were, how did they fandangle this case?

A teaser to these troubling inquiries is provided by the Tanner ruckus. But before we go to her evidence, we ought to step back and be clear what we're talking about.

Through Tanner the abductor is conjured back into existence. Through Tanner we time travel backwards through Amaral's dismissal, the McCann's return to Rothley, the McCanns fingered as Arguidos, Gerry's flight to Washington, Kate's dream, Krugel's tricorder coming to the rescue, we move beyond the McCanns move to the villa, their visits to Clement Freud's mansion, flights to Rome, until finally they move from 4G back to 5A.

What we also want to see is how Tanner's narrative impacted on the real-time narrative. What happened when Robert Murat was cleared? What happened to the credibility of Tanner's sighting then?

To be clear, we need to understand Tanner's involvement, and Tanner's sighting from the vantage point of what a real abduction should or would look like. How ought the victims to deal with this potentially crucial lead? What should the police do? How should both parties work with the witness to see justice done? And what about the abductor? What to do when your name, clothes and even how you walk is wall to wall in the media? What do you do?

We also want to backtrack and join the timeline within the context of a genuine investigation. What would a genuine investigation look like with everyone on board? The media, instead of an intimate partner and enabler is back to its role as a fly on the wall. The McCanns and cops in this ideal scenario are partners. Tanner is eager to help, as are the others in the Tapas seven. In this scenario, the media might still be useful. But what and how to use the horn if you could? If you had it at your beck and call?

Had the McCanns truly been invested in the efforts of the Polícia Judiciária, and had the secrecy laws been a legitimate issue, surely it would have made more sense for both parties to selectively and strategically leak their best clues to the media. Do you follow? Both sides were leaking. Leaks were happening anyway so why not work together on leaking what mattered most in the most effective way possible?

This suggests a collaborative effort between the McCanns and cops, but...to what end? Well, to manipulate, intimidate and flush out *the abductor*! Remember him?

As you're about to see, this is hardly as farcical as it sounds because ultimately the faux abductor *was* flushed out, thanks to Jane Tanner. Tanner's leaks *were* sufficient for him [introduced imminently as "Mr. Khaki"] to be agitated out of anonymity and to say to the world and the media:

Hey, I'm that guy!

[Well he *was* but he wasn't the "abductor"].

Now leave me the hell alone!

But this assumes the cops believed there was an abductor out there. So, did they?

Whatever they believed, it seems clear early on that the cops didn't see eye to eye with the McCanns. [Ditto the cops and the Ramseys]. If the McCanns, like the Ramseys, decided from the get go to write off the cops, wasn't the best way to go to hire their own investigators [as the Ramseys did] and flood the media narrative with *actual* progress in their investigation?

In other words, wasn't their best bet to prioritise getting a profile of their suspect – including an <u>identikit</u> – out there as a matter of urgency?

As it turns out, within three days the police did have images of three suspects [known as e-fits], but those pesky secrecy laws prohibited them from publicising them. The thing is, because the McCanns were British, they – well, the British media – sort of *weren't* beholden to the same prohibitions of expression.

From <u>shakedowntitle.com</u>:

...the only image Portuguese police circulated was a picture described as nothing more than an "egg with hair". They said they could not release any images because of secrecy laws and the fear of prejudicing any further investigation.

But a friend of the McCanns said: "It is frankly outrageous that information relating to potential suspects was not made available as a matter of extreme urgency once it was clear what had happened. The early stages of this were crucial and the police of all people should know that. Seeing these images has come as a shock to everyone concerned."

The e-fits emerged as the public prosecutor overseeing the case heavily criticised the police, describing their actions as an "enormous margin of error".

So maybe the police bumbled; what did the McCanns do about it? What I mean is if the police didn't release identikits *did the McCanns care about it then?* If they did care, did they camp out on the police porch, did they bang down doors? Because the flip side of the story was if the police didn't do something, and if they were hamstringing an investigation [for some unknown reason] then what prevented the McCanns from doing their own investigation and releasing their own perp profiles? [As late as 2013, British investigators released yet another set of e-fits].

Think about it from the McCann's perspective. If you want to catch someone you're going to go from one end of the rumor mill to the other, picking up information and deciding what is actionable. The most obvious information of course didn't come from the other side of the Algarve, or even the other side of Praia da Luz. It didn't even come from the other side of the Ocean Club.

As it turned out, the witness [who conveniently doubled as Gerry McCann's alibi] *came to the McCanns* and the McCanns...did...what? It's not entirely clear what they did with the information, other than mention it in Kate's book that appeared in 2011. Perhaps it wasn't especially important information?

Jane Tanner was a friend of the McCanns, and according to Jane, she'd seen a dodgy dude in khaki trousers at 21:15 carrying a child who was apparently wearing matching pajamas [matching Madeleine's that is].

"Not wanting to alarm" Kate, Jane and Gerry didn't mention Mr Khaki to Madeleine's mother that night. Despite the hotel erupting into a pandemonium of searching for an *anonymous* someone, and despite Kate apparently staying awake most of the time, Jane and Gerry decided to leave mentioning Mr. Khaki until later. A swathe of Praia da Luz had also left their beds to do the same. Wouldn't it have been useful to know what the hell they were looking for?

Kate found out about Mr. Khaki from Tanner later that morning, and was "relieved" when she heard the news.

In the Ramsey case this weird word also vomits into view at the most bizarre moment. When John Ramsey discovers his dead daughter in the basement he's "relieved" as no innocent parent on Earth would be under similar circumstances.

Similarly, to hear word critical hours after one's daughter's abduction [if that's what it was], of a phantom abductor…well… if Kate really cared about her daughter she would have been devastated.

Oh my God, so she was taken…

And she would be desperate to know everything about her abductor, what he looked like, how old he was, his demeanour, his intent, the way he moved…to try to intuit Madeleine's chances.

If Kate really cared about investigating the crime, she would have frogmarched Jane to the cop shop and not rested until the picture in Tanner's mind was flashing in the sky for all to see in Praia da Luz.

I want to emphasise that if the McCanns wanted to put together an identikit, there were no geographical or language barrier preventing them from doing so, all they had to do was ask Jane.

So, did they? And if they didn't, what did *Jane* do?

We know that Jane's first interview[64] with *any* newspaper was with *The Sun* on [wait for it] 20 November 2007. For reasons unknown, Jane had sat on apparently vital information for seven months. Since the

---

64 Jane Tanner was interviewed by the police on May 10th, 2007.

McCanns were official suspects thanks to sniffer dogs, it was important to bring the abductor back into the narrative.

From shakedowntitle.com:

"I DID see a man that night carrying away Madeleine. She WAS abducted[65]*...Every day I see him there, striding away, carrying Madeleine and I try desperately to remember more detail, what his face was like. I think about it over and over again. It's horrible... Every day I hope this is the day we find her."*

But then why wait seven months to talk about it?

From shakedowntitle.com:

Twisting her Look For Madeleine yellow and green wristbands, Jane, 36, then went into detail about the night of May 3...she saw a man cross from left to right in front of her with a child lolling back in his arms...It wasn't unusual to see people with children, even at that time of night. But my attention was drawn to him because the child had bare feet... ***It was a cold night*** *and I thought that was strange because as a mother I would never have taken my child around at that time without something on their feet or a blanket. All I could see of the child was their legs dangling. The man was about ten to fifteen feet in front of me and was* ***walking quite quickly*** *and I can remember thinking, 'That's odd'.*

Let's flashback quickly to Gerry McCann's statement to the cops:

"I opened the children's door 60 degrees and looked to the left and saw Maddie sleeping with her head on the pillow on the right-hand side of the bed. She was breathing softly and I thought how beautiful she looked. I ***thought it was quite hot*** *and I didn't need to cover her up."*

---

65 According to certain witnesses interviewed by Joseph Moura, a private investigator, Jane Tanner never left the Tapas bar on May 3rd, 2007.

Jane Tanner makes an interesting admission here, though. She says even at around 21:00 it wasn't unusual to see people ferrying their kids to hotel rooms. Remember, this was a resort town and unlike the McCanns, a lot of holidaymakers were making use of crèche facilities while having their dinners. And so once done, obviously, they would carry their children back to their beds.

Do you see the mismatch in Tanner's statement?

It wasn't unusual < > It was strange

Which was it then? Why was it odd that a father would be walking quickly on a cold night?

Of course, if the man was in front of her, Jane wouldn't be able to get a good look at his face. So, despite her brilliant vigilance, it would be a faceless identikit when it was eventually compiled, which is about as useful as an ejection seat on a helicopter.

From shakedowntitle.com:

*"I never at that time thought it could be Madeleine. **I'd just passed Gerry** so I thought his children were all asleep in bed." Jane said the first she knew [something was wrong] was when she looked out of her window and saw the table at the tapas bar was empty. She opened the door and there was commotion.*

…"Rachael, shouted at me, 'Madeleine's gone!' As soon as she said that the image of that man carrying the child came into my head and I felt physically sick. A feeling of complete horror washed over me."

…I never thought it could be Madeleine < > As soon as she said 'Madeleine's gone!' the image of the man carrying the child came into my head…

Which was it then?

And Jane Tanner is so convinced of her story she decides not to tell Kate immediately but let her cry and worry without offering anything of value. Not only would one mother never do this to another mother, what about poor Madeleine? Did it make sense to protect her mother's *feelings* during an emergency in which Madeleine's life was at stake?

From shakedowntitle.com:

*Minutes later Jane saw Kate. Close to tears, Jane admitted she could not bear to tell her about the man. She said: "At that time it seemed everyone thought Madeleine was hiding. I knew that if I told her about the man **it would shatter that**. I was also hoping desperately that I'd been wrong. Instead I took another friend, Fiona, to one side and told her."*

According to Tanner, she informed the police at "around 23:15". While Tanner and the McCanns maintain the police took hours to arrive on the scene, the police themselves indicate they arrived 10-15 minutes after being summoned. Given the size of Praia da Luz, there's no reason to suspect otherwise, but we'll make absolutely sure of timelines in due course.

In any event Tanner relates how the police walked her through the sighting and then it struck her – *the pyjamas were a perfect match for Madeleine's.* In a way, it was a perfect clusterfuck too – Tanner had seen virtually everything:

1. An abduction.
2. A positive I.D. on Madeleine's pyjamas[66] [and thus Madeleine herself]
3. Gerry McCann not carrying anyone.
4. An I.D. on the clothing of the abductor.

---

66 In fact it wasn't a positive ID on Madeleine's pyjamas at all. These were Mr. Khaki's daughter's pyjamas. These were Madeleine's. Positive match?

The only thing missing was the abductor dude.

According to Jane: *"He had his face turned away and it was dark."*

Strange that because if Tanner could see the child's bare feet, and the child was being carried with the head away from the viewer, then it suggested she could see him at least in profile. Also, if he was walking fast, this ought to have changed the angle from which she saw him.

The bottom line of course is that Tanner's identikit seems to have been produced only in November 2007, if one reads between the lines. Besides that, Tanner – despite being tortured daily with these memories – apparently didn't think to contact the authorities about it either, which is why the article appeared to prompt the Polícia Judiciária to get in touch with Tanner.

From shakedowntitle.com:

"I've done an artist's impression and want people to look at that and rack their brains as to whether they know him, or if they were on holiday, saw him."...Meanwhile, the Portuguese police plan to question the McCanns; seven friends once more, it was reported today.

Portuguese newspaper Jornal de Noticias said the interviews would take place in an attempt to clear up some of the reported contradictions in the friends' statements.

It's easy to criticise Tanner's testimony and her timing, but the real issue is the McCann's. In Kate's book, she reveals that Gerry knew about Mr Khaki before she did [on the night of May 3rd] and that by morning [May 4th], Kate herself knew about Mr. Khaki. Wouldn't it have been more constructive to pursue Mr Khaki as a lead rather than launching balloons or mass producing wrist bands?

What I mean is, if Mr Khaki was a real breakthrough, then why worry about the PR. Go after your abductor!

In any event, for whatever reason the McCanns were preoccupied with other things and we now know, in hindsight, that Mr Khaki remained a "prime suspect" for six long years.

Suffice it to say, from a certain perspective, Mr Khaki remaining a suspect *may have been helpful* to the McCanns.

In the end, Mr Khaki did eventually come forward. Although he'd shat himself for six long years given the ongoing media holocaust, Mr Khaki came forward *of his own volition*, and even showed the clothes he'd worn that fateful night.

The point is, if Mr Khaki really was prime suspect material, he could have and should have been exposed from the get go. Why did it take six years to flush him out? His story and description could have been pinned to those balloons and on WANTED posters pasted throughout the Algarve. Kate and Gerry could have started and ended every news conference with reminders that this was their best lead. Identikits could have been burned into the pitches of those soccer and cricket stadiums. But what would that have achieved? It would have *cleared* Mr Khaki within the first days or weeks and perhaps that didn't suit a particular narrative...

Had <u>a concerted effort been made to mislead?</u>

This is the *flaw* in running to the media rather than working with the police, and both sides collaborating with the media in the conducting of an earnest investigation. Hold on. *Flaw* doesn't seem like the right word, does it? *Agenda* somehow feels better. There is a sense of an *appearance* of effort and the *appearance* of indignation. Following the Tanner sighting, and identikit, there are dozens of additional sightings that don't amount to anything and thus, much ado about nothing. Which is why this, from a "friend" of the McCanns, rings rather hollow:

"It is frankly outrageous that information relating to potential suspects was not made available as a matter of extreme urgency once it was clear what had happened."

If the McCanns themselves were sitting on the Tanner sighting, why was it allowed to stew in true crime oblivion for six years? Think about what Mr Khaki had to go through once a cartoon of himself was put on the radar – it was enough to fan the media narrative but not enough to add to the actual investigation. If the Polícia Judiciária's "egg with hair" was absurd, Tanner's "egg abductor in khaki trousers" was no better.

And Mr Khaki himself, the only man in the world who knew the cartoon referred to him, also knew something else: he knew the child in his arms that night was *his* child. Mr Khaki probably reasoned that if he stayed on the side-lines, sanity would eventually prevail. He was wrong.[67]

---

67 As noted, in 2013 – after enduring six years of accusations – Mr Khaki, a British father eventually came forward and rubbished Tanner's allegations against him. By the time he did, the "abductor" narrative had been fully absorbed into the mythology surrounding Madeleine's "mysterious" disappearance.

~

Two Psychological Postcards from South Africa [Part one]

"We've obviously looked at evidence about cadaver dogs and they're incredibly unreliable."
— <u>Gerry McCann during a November 2009 television interview</u> with Portuguese journalist Sandra Felgueira

The 1991 film *The Doctor,* starring William Hurt, is excellent psychological fodder for the McCann case. We may assume because both parties in this case are doctors that we know what we're dealing with. Do we really?

Doctors are typically well-to-do, intelligent and genuine people, right? I'm <u>not sure if that is entirely accurate</u>. And <u>here's why</u>. Certain doctors [<u>especially surgeons</u>[68]] require degrees of psychopathy to fit their job description.

In a sense this lack of emotion is potentially a defense mechanism, used to separate the patient and the painful realities that come from getting too close to patients [who may die] from the doctor.

---

68 <u>Dr. David Payne, one of the Tapas Seven, was a surgeon.</u>

In *The Doctor,* we see some of the implications of that uncaring psychopathy, where people's lives are literally on the line. Their fate may be decided by the whims of their doctor. And when doctor Jack McKee [William Hurt] falls ill with throat cancer and finds himself on the receiving end of that psychopathy, he's truly terrified.

Try to intuit the emotion loaded into these quotes from the movie.

Dr. Eli Blumfield: *I've always wanted to slit your throat, and now I get a chance to.*

Here's more from the movie plot from imdb.com:

Jack McKee is a doctor with it all: he's successful, he's rich, extremely self-centred and he has no problems…he realises that there is more to life than serving only his own needs…

Being married to a doctor [and both Kate and Gerry were] might involve dealing with a special brand of selfish narcissism, and with that comes…what?

Anne MacKee: *You know, it's funny. I wake up every morning, and I have this… this feeling. This sensation. And I didn't know what it was. What is it? Am I hungry? Am I tired? Am I sad? Then I realized… I'm just lonely.*

Once upon a time I had an affair with a Scottish doctor, an anaesthetist. She was married, I wasn't. She was also into running. She didn't want to have children. She, like me, declared herself too selfish for that. I naively assumed that her attraction to me was sort've borne out of dissatisfaction with her significant other [who also happened to be a doctor].

Over a couple of weeks, I got to know her schedule and became increasingly aware of the weird hours she worked as a doctor. She often pulled long and lonely night shifts, and if I was up and working [as

I often was], we might share an intimate discussion throu
hours.

Since anaesthetists are doctors that advise other doctors, she
was – as one might expect – super-smart and very well read, which
I enjoyed. I enjoyed talking to her. We enjoyed other things too. I
learnt a terrific amount from her. But when weekend after weekend
went into quality time with her husband, it started to sink in what
was happening. I was an object of convenience; a consumable, a
pick-me-up on a down day. Okay maybe I was a little more than that,
but not much more. Whatever I was, I was being masterfully slotted
into and out of her life. My attention wavered. When she became
more demanding, the genie suddenly slipped out of the bottle and
everything fizzled.

It meant something to me, still does, but there was something very
superior and very selfish about where she was coming from. There was a
real decadence brewing just below the surface of a respectable lifestyle.
What is a respectable lifestyle these days? It was hard to say exactly what
it was but there was *something* troubling about the ease in which I could
be ushered in and out of her life, which meant just as I might be an
object of convenience, I could also be disposed of, and I was.

Many people see doctors as a privileged class, part of an elite. Doctors
in turn seem to take to their better-than-you pedestals with aplomb. But
I don't think the way to intuit the psychology of doctors is going to
bring this case any closer. Thinking about them as some recondite alien
species isn't the way to untangle this knot.

The way to really understand psychopathy is when we acknowledge
it *in ourselves*. When we acknowledge our own lack of compassion,
our own merciless selfishness, we begin to see a terrifying potential for
harm in others too.

Shall I go first? During the course of writing this narrative, Lisa Wilson, my Los Angeles-based partner in crime writing revealed a close friend of hers had been diagnosed with stage four cancer. What is there to say or feel when someone you don't know falls terminally ill? 24 hours later another friend Whatsapped me with news that her mother had died. What can one say beyond I'm sorry? To be honest, I didn't really slow down my work rate and attend to either of them, and Lisa later accused me of <u>lacking compassion</u>.

When I climbed Kilimanjaro with my older brother he got into trouble on the last day and what did I do? I forged ahead. He got to the top, no thanks to me, but I guess I could have done better. We all can, right? But if we can all *be* better, why aren't we? Why are some of us prone to be real sons [and daughters] of bitches? <u>Being a shithead, if one's not careful, can become a habit</u>, and an ugly one.

By the way, the same charts that have surgeons ranking in psychopathy have journalists right up there too. And I have to admit, sometimes I am so wrapped up in "narrative" I have trouble linking hands with real life, in the real world, right now. It's not an excuse, and it's not right but it is true.

How about you?

What troubles us about the McCann case is not merely the possibility of a single merciless parent, but two and perhaps even a group. Through Madeleine we acknowledge our own inner child, and see how at any moment a life that thought it meant something, belonged somewhere, could have been discarded and dumped without so much as a flicker of genuine sadness afterwards.

In their media appearances that followed Madeleine's disappearance, the McCanns claimed they'd been advised not to look emotional as this could gratify the criminal that had their daughter. Well, both parents were masterful in keeping a tight lid on their excessive emotions, weren't they?

If we need to address our own capacities to psychopathy as a pathway to intuiting the McCann's psychology [and *potential* psychopathy], in other areas we must remember who we are dealing with.

Doctors habitually deal with issues of mortality. Body parts fail, so do human beings. Shit happens. Doctors are habitually confronted with the chore of healing failing human tissues. Sometimes they win, sometimes they lose.

They may examine lumps of flesh [rather than people], inject it [rather than them] and yes, be involved in disposing of it. It's a bad joke that doctors bury their failures. But disposal is a daily regimen for doctors, especially hospital staff [and Gerry was that in 2007]. Syringes and surgical equipment must be sterilized and incinerated on a daily basis. Hands are washed on an hourly basis. Doctors, more so than most, are aware of tissue damage, discoloration, haemorrhage and contamination.

If we are to interrogate all alleyways, even the darkest, in this case, we must ponder the practicalities of what two brilliant but possibly conniving personalities might be capable of. How might a really smart person who is used to disposing of human tissue do so at a holiday resort? Why would they go to so much trouble?

I have seen criminal profilers give massive priority to the McCann's Catholic beliefs. The overriding theme of these suppositions is that the McCanns would want to give their daughter a proper burial. I find this reasoning completely off, because at the core of the McCanns isn't church, but hospitals. These people are doctors through and through, not Catholics through and through. If they were more Catholics than they were doctors, would Madeleine have come to harm in the first place? If they were more Catholics than they were doctors, would there have been a disappearing act to begin with?

It's hard to be sure, but we have to follow the right psychological path from the get go. The doctor psychology gets us part of the way, no doubt, and in my opinion, further than the Catholic psychology does.

Although, hang on, the clergy also make the psychopathy hot list, as do sales folk, CEOs, lawyers and cops.[69] What about you? Be honest.

These days Gerry McCann [professor, actually] conducts medical trials. But human beings aren't guinea pigs. They're not a means to an end.

As for Kate, she conducts ~~choirs~~…Kate is ~~The Missing People's choir~~ a charity ambassador. Kate may be making an appearance affiliated with The Missing People's charity in mid-April 2017, just ahead of the ten-year anniversary of Madeleine's disappearance. A PR coup for Simon Powell, a previous donor to the Find Madeleine Fund, and a coup for the McCanns perhaps?

As recently as March 2017 Gerry was called on to advise on a high-profile heart surgery. That story made national headlines in Britain too. The well-to-do doctor doing good. All good, right?

Amidst the ongoing warm and fuzzy, feel-good PR surrounding *that* particular surgery and Gerry's central role in it, a "cruel irony" was noted in the same fluffy story. Although Gerry's job is to save the lives of strangers, "he has no idea if his own child who vanished aged three is dead or alive."

But what if he *does* know?

---

69 Jane Tanner was a marketing manager in 2007. John Ramsey was a CEO of a large company when his daughter was murdered. Rachael Oldfield was a former lawyer.

Doubt

"When in doubt tell the truth." — Mark Twain

If there's any doubt that doctors are not more sensitive than our fellow human beings but less, <u>there's a great article</u> published in the *New Yorker* [April 2017] written by a doctor. An oncologist. Oncologists spend their lives trying to separate human beings from tumours, but over time, seem to struggle to separate living tissue from globs of diseased gunk.

The theme of the entire piece is numbness and desensitization.

From <u>newyorker.com</u>:

Numbness, you might say, is my occupational hazard. Over the past month or so, I have watched twelve of my patients die from or relapse with cancer...When interviewers ask me how I carry on carrying on, I speak about... startling successes [and] about hope and the future. But I do not—I cannot—tell them that a certain kind of numbness must be a part of it. I come home from the bone-marrow-transplant wards on a January morning and play with my dog, rearrange the furniture, and practice polynomial factorization with my daughter. I celebrate a recent laboratory paper with a glass of champagne. I return to the wards the next morning... to find a marrow choked up with leukemia cells... And this cycle repeats. You might say that I have an advanced degree in desensitization.

Now, why would this guy admit that he does not and cannot talk about the numbness that comes with the territory of being a doctor? Well, the reason is obvious, isn't it? Would you go to a doctor that wasn't sensitive to you, whether you lived or died, whether you were in pain or not? Would you put your health and wellbeing in the hands of someone who could care less? No one would!

But if there's a numbness that afflicts the medical profession [and there is], there is also a numbness that afflicts and surrounds us today.

From newyorker.com:

How shall we continue to write in these numbing times?... The gaze [must be] unsparing and penetrating, clear-eyed, clinical...[you] cannot see if your eyes are clouded with tears...a weeping doctor is a useless doctor. He cuts away the artifice. He cauterizes our indulgences in pity or piety: it is impossible, he reminds us, to feel pity for the self-pitying.

And so, in the Algarve, we find a group of doctors in disarray. Mark Twain speaks of telling the truth when in doubt, but did they? Twain also refers to there being "no surer way to find out whether you like people or hate them than to travel with them."

We have travelled through time with the McCanns and in all this time, do we ever see a weeping doctor?

...a weeping doctor is a useless doctor...

The doubt that plagues the McCanns, at least the way I see it, is amorphous in some ways. There's nothing clinical or scientific about it. Stirring in the emptiness of our own humanity seems to be a recognition that something is missing in theirs. What though?

Well, how about compassion?

What about honesty and authenticity?

Doctors are smart and invariably charming, but what we don't like to entertain is what festers beneath the cool, polished façade of intelligence, efficacy and excellence? There's a certain heartlessness, isn't there?

I do not—I cannot—tell them that a certain kind of numbness must be a part of it.

And so, in a sense, all doctors must be liars. They lie to others and they lie to themselves. But, so do we. Do we like to acknowledge the ever-present reality of death? Do we like to admit that our own destruction is almost always imminent? So, in a sense we are all liars, though some of us lie and feel nothing as part of our job descriptions.

What on Earth is the way out of this monstrous dilemma? Is there a way up and out of this sinking chasm?

From newyorker.com:

[But then] the clinical detachment...gives way to tenderness...the patient cannot be left to wither under the mercury bulbs. She must be tended and resuscitated, made whole again. It is easy for the doctor to express moral outrage or indignation [at the affliction]... but there is narcissism in that revulsion. It is easy, too, to concoct a moral fable out of sickness...but there is sadism in that confabulation. It is vastly more difficult, and more courageous, to observe, describe, diagnose, empathize, and heal... [It is] —compassion—that moves us beyond numbness toward healing.

In the McCann case, if we are to find healing, we must tell the truth, or try.

We begin this process by opening our hearts and minds to the raven, and allowing a great darkness to spill through us. With it come doubts and uncertainty. Of course, they were already there all the time, just like the darkness was. The only difference is, we are now in a position where we open the door – well, ourselves – to the darkness. We make ourselves vulnerable to it, and there is an exchange that happens. The life force is contaminated by the ether and the shadows that lurk in it. And the shadow is transmuted to…well…

It is easy, too, to concoct a moral fable out of sickness…

Are we sure that's what really happened here? I think it's fair to say that we are not, and the lingering and looming doubts are why this episode has defied denouement for as long as it has.

That there are doubts is clear, but what is less clear is exactly what they are. So, let's be explicit about them. Let's draw them out of the shadows and try to shine something on them, try to see what's under these shapeshifting mind games. Shall we?

We see symptoms of this in Kate McCanns recent removal from The Missing Person choir. Not removal really as much as renaming. Endlessly trying to find a more suitable, a more appropriate catechism. That Kate McCann finds herself in 2017 unable to be seen as a genuine ambassador for The Missing People choir speaks volumes. We do not like to admit it, but the real reason for this is there are growing doubts about Kate's claims. How can you have someone represent the cause of missing people when the authenticity of your own missing child is in doubt. And that's what it comes down to. Was Madeleine ever *really* missing?

There's bitter irony in the most reported missing person's case in modern history washing up ten years later as potentially a hoax. Did any of that saturation media coverage consider possible alternatives?

Below is a list of Twelve Doubts that we have examined thus far. How many have been resolved to satisfaction? And where do these Twelve Doubts eventually lead us?

1. Is <u>Madeleine actually alive and living in plain sight</u>, as the media currently speculate, but she doesn't know she's missing?

2. Both <u>prime suspects identified in this case</u> [Murat and "Mr. Khaki'] associated with "abduction" sightings on May 3rd have proved to be bogus. So, are there no suspects in Madeleine's disappearance?

3. The McCanns claim they have alibis for the night in question thanks to <u>the Tapas Seven</u>. Are <u>the witness testimonies of the Tapas Seven</u>, essentially confirmations of the McCann's version, <u>actually credible</u>? In other words, do the McCanns have alibis?

4. What was <u>the actual implication of Madeleine saying to her parents</u>: "Where were you last night when we were crying...?"

5. If the McCann children were sedated, why would the McCanns further inconvenience themselves by checking on them every 20 minutes or so?

6. Did Gerry return from his check <u>at 21:25 as some members of the Tapas Seven have suggested he did</u>, and was a meal really waiting to be served as Gerry and the Tapas Seven claim there was?

7. If Madeleine wasn't sedated and if she was abducted, if the Tanner or Smith sightings were genuine, then <u>why was Madeleine still asleep while being carried away</u> by a stranger? Why didn't she make a sound or struggle against her abductor?

8. <u>Was the man in the Smith sighting walking towards the sea</u>, or a church? <u>Who was that man</u> and when exactly was the man sighted?

9. If the McCanns were involved, where on Earth could they have hidden Madeleine when the window of opportunity to slip away and return was minimal?

10. <u>Was Madeleine buried in the construction site of a parking lot beside the church</u>, and is that why she's never been found?

11. <u>If Madeleine is dead, where are her remains</u>? Were her remains moved, and if so, when, how and by who?

12. <u>Are Madeleine's remains still in Praia da Luz</u> or somewhere else? If the little girl was dumped or hidden somewhere in the resort town, wouldn't the summer flocks that followed in May, June and July eventually have caught whiff of her decaying remains? Would hiding her remains in a car, even temporarily, have kept Madeleine hidden from the public?

In late February 2017 television investigator Mark Williams-Thomas appeared on *ITV's This Morning* to expound on his latest theory. Through our various narratives we've encountered Williams-Thomas before. His exclusive coverage of the Oscar Pistorius case was, I thought, opportunistic and his reinforcement and validation of Oscar's half-baked version of events less than convincing.

On the McCann case, however, I think he does a little better.

From shakedowntitle.com:

[Williams-Thomas] echoed previously reported lines about Maddie's asking her mum and dad "Where were you last night?" and her twin siblings waking up on previous nights.

He then stated: "The concern I have, I believe she woke up and went looking for them, she left the apartment and came out, we already know the patio door was insecure."

The implication is that Madeleine was subsequently snatched by an opportunistic predator. Of course, on this theory the McCanns come off looking like even more negligent parents. Madeleine's awake and walking the streets alone at night. Where are her parents?

Interestingly the McCann's spokesman, Clarence Mitchell, has responded to Williams-Thomas.

From shakedowntitle.com:

"This is pure speculation and as such Kate and Gerry will not be dignifying it with any sort comment whatsoever."

Well, except he just did.

From shakedowntitle.com:

A source close to the pair said: "It's baffling a television programme had him on as an authority on the Madeleine case. He's re-invented himself as a criminologist but when did he become an expert on this high profile case? Never!"

There are elements of truth in Williams-Thomas' assertion, I think, but also elements of truth in Clarence Mitchell's response to it. There is insight and keen speculation. But there is also baffling befuddlement. In other words, there is still plenty of doubt raging through the British press ten years after the fact. If there's no consensus now, will there ever be?

Is there any way through the endless veils of darkness and doubt?

The way out of the doctor's dilemma – the cloying anaesthesia – is the anaesthetic. Yes, the totemic black fire of the raven.

Motive & Method

"Man is a substance clad in shadows."
— John Sterling

The raven stands beside a puddle. Though the world is a fading winter forest without the sun, a triangle of light sits in the slanted slab below the fishermen's huts. A bulb from one of those huts is reflected in the water, turning it into a golden mirror.

Don't look, listen.

Listen to what?

The mercury surface trembles as though a beast, a dinosaur, approaches. Then in the whisper of wind on water are the words…

…the one is the other…

And then the mirror is still. The fisherman's light that has burned all night is suddenly extinguished.

Don't listen, sniff.

We smell the air. It is rich with the salt of the North Atlantic, and the sun-baked dust of the Sahara. Just across the roiling waters are endless oceans of sand.

The raven erupts into the air and lands on our shoulder.

After a moment, it shifts from one leg to the other.

...the one is the other...

What could it possibly mean?

I turn back to the puddle which, with the lights out, has disappeared in the murk. One could hardly know there was water there, or anything wet if one hadn't seen it. But if you can't see the mirror and can't hear it and can't smell it, what good is it?

It's a psychological mirror...

The words from the raven are warm and close and clear. We can feel its serrated edges but not the way it cuts.

Cuts both ways...

There is a bizarre guffaw [or a cough] from the road as a late-night Romeo returns to his roost. A shadow returning to bed before break of day.

Don't look, listen.

We close our eyes and over the slow sighing of the sea is the sound of breathing. It advances and then retreats. And then again, breathing... coming closer...and then disappearing. There is also a soft *scruff scruff scruff* that comes and goes with the breathing...

They are joggers, running along the narrow fisherman's road. It is a one-way ribbon of road winding along the rocky coast. It is also their running route.

It's a psychological mirror...

...the one is the other...

~ 219 ~

We reach through the cloying anaesthesia, through the brewing amnesia for the aesthetic in the ether. The raven, as if connected by thought, or some intercom system to the mind, answers.

Yes, all things are connected. The one is the other, and what we must do here, is connect the one psychological mirror to the other.

It is <u>like floating</u> across the dark side of the moon. Floating over rock and high rise. Floating over ink black roads and vehicles polished by night. We're on the sloping incline of Rua Dr Francisco Gentil Martins again.

…connect the one psychological mirror to the other…

The raven flaps in a low arc and then alights on a stop sign. Barely discernible are the words "McCann Circus"<u> stencilled under the word</u> <u>STOP</u>. The scarlet paint of the sign is a dull grey in this near complete absence of light.

The raven shakes its feathers and bobs its head and just then, inspiration – like lightning – strikes.

Think of the psychological symbolism in the Tapas Seven narrative that took place over about an hour on the night of May 3rd, and the entire Find Madeleine narrative which followed on the morning after, and continues to this day.

…the one is the other…

The one is a smaller version of the other.

<u>The Tapas Seven and the McCanns and the hotel staff are on one</u> <u>side</u>. On the other is Madeleine, who is perhaps sedated. Connecting the one to the other are various appearances by various players. Like threads spinning from cotton reels, one thread after another rolls out to tie the Tapas restaurant to the little girl in her bed. One of the Tapas Seven gets up to "search" for Madeleine, to make sure she is okay. Then

the next, in a constant relay. At the beginning and end of this relay are the McCanns themselves. In the middle are others – other doctors, other agents, others who can speak for them.

That is the microcosm for what follows.

...connect the one psychological mirror to the other...

On the one side are the McCanns, the Tapas Seven, ambassadors, lawyers, marketers and the media. On the other is Madeleine, who is perhaps ~~sedated~~ dead. Connecting the one to the other are various appearances by various players. Like threads spinning from cotton reels, one thread after another rolls out to tie the McCanns as loving parents to their daughter, and sightings to an abductor. One after another are events to commemorate or keep Madeleine alive. There is one investigation after another, but as the tricorder shows, these aren't genuine investigations. The suspects identified in the sightings aren't genuine either. Just as the checks weren't genuine. There is a constant relay to keep up the appearance of searching for Madeleine, wanting to find Madeleine. At the beginning and end of this relay are the McCanns themselves. In the middle are others – police, lawyers, spindoctors, fundraisers, others who can speak for them.

Put simply:

Tapas Seven + McCanns + keeping up appearance of checking = Madeleine sedated

World Media + police + Tapas Nine + Search PR [not a genuine search] = Madeleine dead

On the other side of the equation is nothing. Nothing for human beings, at least.

Don't listen, sniff.

For dogs there seems to be something; is it the unmistakable smell of a cadaver? And does that smell belong to Madeleine, or what remains of her?

Since the far side of the equation is darkness, everything must be engineered and rejigged on the other side to keep the equation in play. Essentially the left side of the equation endlessly plays with and recycles itself. It is the same information that repeats in different guises, just as the Tapas Seven and the McCanns looking in on Madeleine is repeated on a grander stage; the stage of Portugal and Britain, the tabloid media, newspapers, football matches and fundraisers. There are urgent events and prayers, anniversaries and missing person's fairs, but no real investigation, no real leads, no real Madeleine.

Has a concerted effort been made to mislead?

If there has, what is it that we aren't supposed to see?

...connect the one psychological mirror to the other...

...the one is the other...

Smith saw something, didn't he? And of all the players in this game, Smith doesn't read like an agent [perhaps because he's from Ireland].

So, what did he see?

Don't look, listen.

It's a psychological mirror...

...the one is the other...

Haven't we been down this road before though? The Tapas on the one side and Madeleine sedated on the other is a mirror for...

The raven flaps impatiently off the stop sign and <u>plonks onto the</u> <u>smooth cool, down-sloping tar of Rua Dr Francisco Gentil Martins</u>. The raven beckons, motions with its beak and strides and hops along the road and then skips onto the sidewalk. <u>Right to the small gate below 5A.</u> Right where the raven first brought us.

Don't look, listen.

It's a psychological mirror…

…the one is the other…

<u>Haven't we been down these steps before?</u>

Yes, and so have they.

…the one is the other…

<u>It's just an ordinary staircase</u>. Narrow. High white walls, if you're a four-year-old otherwise not very high. <u>Gates</u> on <u>either end</u>.

Don't look, listen.

"…we barely used the front door, coming and going through the patio doors and up and down the steps…."

<u>Listen…</u>

And then, there it is.

The other psychological mirror…

"…up and down the steps…."

<u>Two parents</u>, <u>three children</u>, <u>up and down the steps</u>.

<u>Are you sure you want to hear this?</u>

With two small children and the only access they used up and down a staircase, this would have meant Madeleine would have [probably] been left to walk up and down herself. This "exercise" may have prompted her, on the night after crying to no avail, to go and search for mummy and daddy. If the patio door was unlocked, <u>did the balcony gate need to be</u>? And if various Tapas visitors had come in, had they remembered to secure the gate after them?

Even so, Madeleine may have climbed over it, or managed to unlock it. The combination of being <u>compromised by Calpol</u> and distressed may have undermined her ability to ambulate. Her balance may have been wonky.

To sustain a fatal blow from a fall off the couch is possible, but unlikely. The couch would have had to be a fair distance from the wall, and the couch itself a fair distance from the floor. If toddlers could die from simply falling off couches, the McCanns wouldn't have had to go to the Algarve for that to happen. Couches would come with airbags, and safety nets. They don't because no one falls off a couch; they're designed to be fallen on.

But a three-year-old falling down a flight of stairs, or off the side of the patio balcony [cadaver scent was found directly below the balcony] could be fatal, particularly if it involved a snapping of the neck.

In this scenario, the culpability of both parents, comes into question, and <u>especially parents as doctors</u>. Fiona Payne observed Kate, after Madeleine had vanished, checking to see if her comatose twins were <u>*still breathing*</u>, by placing her fingers repeatedly beside their noses.

In <u>2005, 12 million dosages of infant dosage Calpol were sold in Britain</u>. On the Calpol website today <u>the sleep remedy is given as "routine"</u>. Kate is meticulous in her narrative to stress that this was precisely what they were doing and that it was working.

I don't think it was.

I have always found Kate's anecdote about a large bruise on Madeleine's lower leg extremely odd. Kate herself had several bruises on her forearms too. How did they get them?

If Madeleine did fall down the steps, she and her Cuddle Cat may have been brought inside [possibly by Kate, since Kate's clothing also bingoed with the dogs], and her small corpse hidden temporarily behind the sofa, and then inside the wardrobe in the adults bedroom. Both parents may have rationalised that Madeleine's death had nothing to do with them. She fell. They didn't do anything.

Then they would have waited for darkness to fall in order to do what the Ramseys could not. Remove the little corpse from the room through the other door, and leave it outside, somewhere else. But where?

Don't look, listen.

Another jogger puffs by, heading down to the scenic seaside route beside the fishermen's huts. One way provided a slightly smelly run to the deserted and rocky West end of Praia da Luz. The other, beyond the church, afforded panoramic views of the entire beach and Rocha Negra. It could all be seen at a single glance.

To be assured of a plausible alibi, or at least plausible deniability, it was important to do all this in a co-ordinated fashion so cell phones would have been useful.[70] By inviting their friends into the scenario there was another potential psychological mirror – by becoming witnesses to the incident, including the crime scene – apartment 5A,

---

70 Lingering doubt exists over fourteen SMS messages that appear to have been erased from Gerry McCann's phone during that fateful dinner in the Tapas restaurant on May 3rd.

their alibis became welded to the McCanns. Thus, if things went pear-shaped, their fates were just as much on the line as co-conspirators.[71]

When it was dark <u>it was downhill all the way</u>. And most of <u>the route</u> on <u>that side of town</u> was <u>shuttered</u> or <u>shouldered</u> by <u>the backs of buildings</u>. Who is he carrying?

Madeleine, of course.

A few minutes there, an unfortunate encounter, <u>through to the rocks, a quick jog back</u> and then a change of clothes – out of those beige trousers.

An old, <u>upturned fishing boat near the sewer</u> could serve as a temporary coffin for the dead little girl. Frequent visits to the rocky slab and the church in the days following could test the air for giveaway odours, but fishing on the far side and the increased flushing of sewers during the busy summer period would mask much of it.

Until the tissues and bones could be carted out of Praia da Luz, they would need to be moved again, sealed in a boot, boiling at the end of a driveway. And then at an appointed time, with careful planning and sly execution, perhaps her remains could be secreted out and away. Far beyond straying beachcombers and tourists. But where? And when? And who would dare to be so bold?

There is a slow roar that builds over the moony apartments. Is it the sea? Is it the roar of the Rocha Negra, its volcanic cliffs shuddering at man's cold inhumanity to man? Or is it the roar of the dawn, that moment when the nuclear balloon lifts its orange face over the Algarve?

---

71 The Ramseys also invited friends into their home on the morning of December 26th; these friends unwittingly became co-conspirators if they co-operated with the Ramseys or prime suspects when they didn't.

But the sun is not ready yet. The roar comes from somewhere else. Somewhere…up.

Don't look, listen.

A silver splinter cuts through the inky sky. Between puffy clouds it appears and disappears. The raven, sitting on the steel gate, tilts its head this way and that, listening to the jet claw its way across the sky. And then, bright eyed, it bursts from its white, wrought iron perch.

Then it comes.

Rising slowly, as if emerging like a wounded soldier beneath an explosion of colossal black feathers, the eternal sun seeps through. The dawn finally breaks through the shadow of night blanketing the Algarve. Cigarette yellow and orange flame duel for the horizon. Blackened specks pepper the morning omelette and then the entire heaven is broken by raging black birds.

Acknowledgements

In order to piece together this narrative, we've cast a wide net. We've drawn on information from a number of forums, documentaries and online resources which have been cited, in particular: themaddiecasefiles.com and gerrymccannsblogs.co.uk

We gratefully acknowledge the suggestions and support we've received from our readers while on this shared journey towards justice.

Please report errors, omissions or corrections directly to Lisa at @ lisawJ13.

~

About the Author

Nick van der Leek is the author of over 100 narratives. He has a background in law and photojournalism.

To share your insights with the author, join the Shakedown true crime discussions on Facebook or leave a comment on the Shakedowntitle blog.

DOUBT 2 was published in June 2017.

Join the author's true crime community on Patreon at https://www.patreon.com/TCRS.

Printed in Great Britain
by Amazon

30816861R00136